Robert Thompson

*The Glory of the Temple
and the Stage*

Henry Purcell 1659-1695

THE BRITISH LIBRARY

First published 1995 by
The British Library, Great Russell Street, London WC1B 3DG
on the occasion of the exhibition,
THE GLORY OF THE TEMPLE AND THE STAGE:
HENRY PURCELL 1659-1695
18 November 1995 – 18 February 1996

ISBN 0 7123 0420 7

Designed by Alan Bartram
Typeset in Monotype Garamond by Nene Phototypesetters,
Northampton
Colour origination by York House Graphics, Hanwell
Printed in England by Clifford Press, Coventry

Inside front cover: detail of a map by Willam Morgan of 1681-2
showing the area of Westminster Abbey.
(BL Map Library CRACE PORT.11.58, sheet 13)

Inside back cover: George Vertue, *Survey of Whitehall Made in
1680* [published 1740]. (BL Map Library 3615 (15))

ACKNOWLEDGEMENTS

I would like to thank the staff of The British Library, and of the
other libraries and record offices mentioned in this book, for
their unfailing assistance. I have profited greatly from informal
discussions with many of the authors and editors named in the
Bibliography and from conference papers presented by Bruce
Wood and Andrew Pinnock. A special acknowledgement is due
to Robert Shay, as a number of suggestions in this book reflect
his and my joint research. Above all, I am grateful to Margaret
Laurie, Chairwoman of the Purcell Society Committee, for
invaluable advice and criticism.

R.T.

Contents

5   Preface

7   Introduction

7   Apprenticeship and early mastery: Purcell's career to 1682

18   The Glory of the Temple: 1682-88

23   After the Glorious Revolution: church, court and chamber music, 1689-95

31   The Glory of the Stage: music for the theatre

46   Purcell and publishing

48   Music for St Cecilia's Day

53   The keyboard manuscript

53   Past Master

58   Bibliography

59   Autograph manuscripts by Henry Purcell in The British Library

61   List of exhibits

63   Index

Purcell! the pride and wonder of the age,
The glory of the temple, and the stage.

(Henry Hall: *Orpheus Britannicus*, 1698)

Preface

The 300th anniversary of the death of Henry Purcell, the greatest English composer between the 16th and 20th centuries (and often considered the greatest English composer of all time) has been commemorated widely through live performances, broadcasts, recordings and publications. Thus the aural evidence of his genius has been widely disseminated. It is the British Library's privilege to bring to the public an exhibition which contains a very substantial part of the surviving tangible documentary evidence for his life and work. The opportunity has been taken not only to give a clear idea of his life and work through contemporary documents but especially to bring together on public view, it is believed for the first time, the majority of the extant autograph scores by the composer.

The British Library is fortunate to possess many of these, including two of the 'great score books' of church and chamber music and a particularly exciting landmark in this tercentenary year has been the Library's success in acquiring the first autograph of Purcell's keyboard music ever to come to light. However, perhaps the most valuable aspect of the exhibition is the bringing together of manuscripts and other exhibits from many other British locations. So the Library is immensely grateful for the co-operation of the following lenders:

The Barber Institute of Fine Arts, Birmingham University; the Trustees of the British Museum; the Governing Body of Christ Church, Oxford; the Cobbe Foundation; the Syndics of Fitzwilliam Museum, University of Cambridge; the Guildhall Library and Gresham College, London; the Keeper of the Public Records; the National Portrait Gallery; the Royal Academy of Music; the Royal College of Music; West Sussex County Record Office and the Dean and Chapter of Chichester Cathedral; and the Dean and Chapter of Westminster Abbey.

The Arts Council of England has generously provided a grant to make these loans possible and has also sponsored two recitals which are to take place in connection with the exhibition. The Library would like to thank the Arts Council and its officers Kathryn McDowell and Andrew Pinnock for their warm co-operation.

The Library would also like to thank the Purcell Tercentenary Trust and its Chairman, Lord Armstrong of Ilminster, and Secretary, Dr Curtis Price, for the enthusiastic support which the Trust has provided not only in helping raise funds to secure the Purcell Keyboard Manuscript for the nation but also for a generous grant to support the production of the present book. In connection with both the exhibition and the manuscript the Library has also received advice and support from the Purcell Society for which we are much indebted.

Finally I must thank those who have been directly involved in the preparation of the exhibition itself. Our largest debt of gratitude is to Robert Thompson who undertook being external curator for the project and has acquitted himself admirably as this, his book, well testifies. Within the British Library he has been supported by Chris Banks, Curator of Music Manuscripts in the Music Library, Tim Day, of the National Sound Archive, Alan Sterenberg, of the Exhibitions Office, Shelley Jones of the Department of Manuscripts, David Way of the Publications Office, and many other colleagues.

HUGH COBBE, Music Librarian, The British Library, September 1995

These are to signifie unto you his Ma:ties pleasure that you provide & deliver or cause to be provided and delivered unto Henry Purcell late One of the Children of his Ma:ties Chappell Royall whose voyce is changed & is gon from the Chappell Two suites of playne cloth two hatts & hatt bands foure whole shirts foure halfe shirts Six bands Six paire of Cuffes Six handkerchiefs foure paire of stockins foure paire of shoes & foure paire of Gloves And this shalbe yo.r Warr.t Given vnd.r my hand this 17: day of Decemb.r 1673 Jn the 25 yeare of his Ma:ties Reigne

St Alban

To the Right hono.ble
Ralph Montagu Esq.r Master
of his Ma:ties Greate Wardrobe
or to his Deputy there

Introduction

Henry Purcell, the foremost English composer of his generation and one of the outstanding English musicians of all time, died aged 36 on 21 November 1695. We know only the bare outline of his life and character, but he is the earliest major English composer to have left a substantial and varied body of autograph music manuscripts, and these, together with printed sources and copies made by his colleagues, not only provide an insight into his working practices but also sometimes seem to offer a glimpse of the man behind the music.

Henry Hall, who described Purcell as 'The glory of the temple, and the stage' was his near-contemporary as a Chapel Royal chorister and studied with him under John Blow. Hall was a wretched poet, and the line may simply be the best he could think of to rhyme and scan, but it points to an important division in Purcell's career: for most of the 1680s Purcell's working life revolved around the Chapel Royal and the court of monarchs who claimed divine right, whereas after the Glorious Revolution at the end of 1688 he was mainly concerned with music for the public theatre. Of course there are memorable exceptions to this rule, but Hall's couplet neatly contrasts Purcell's two principal areas of achievement.

Apprenticeship and early mastery: Purcell's career to 1682

No record survives of Purcell's early life. His parents were probably an elder Henry Purcell, who died in 1664, and his wife Elizabeth: after his father's death the boy's upbringing may have been entrusted, at least in part, to his uncle Thomas. Both the older Purcells were court musicians, and Thomas held a number of other court appointments, so it is no surprise to find that the young Henry was trained as a chorister in the Chapel Royal. He would have joined the Chapel around 1668, and must quickly have become aware, if he was not already, of the abilities of his father's musical contemporaries in the Restoration court and of the advantages that a successful court career could bestow even if the salaries were not always paid on time: a group portrait traditionally known as 'The Cabal' is now thought to depict royal musicians of the early 1660s and contains a number of indications, such as the men's clothing, the sword in the right foreground and the presence of a pageboy, of the high status they enjoyed (Plate 1).

1. Warrant to provide clothing for Henry Purcell on his leaving the Chapel Royal, 17 December 1673. (PRO LC5/120)

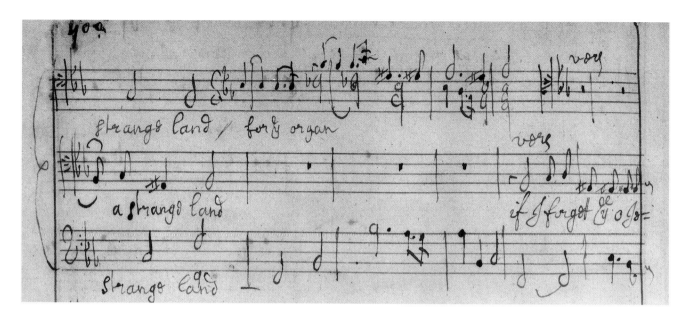

2. Pelham Humfrey, 'By the
waters of Babylon', copied by
Purcell. (BL Add. MS. 30932
f.53v)

OPPOSITE
3. John Blow. A late portrait
from the frontispiece of his
Amphion Anglicus of 1700.
(BL Music Library G.106.)

The earliest evidence we have of Henry Purcell's existence, let alone his musical development, is to be found in three warrants issued in 1673. One appoints him assistant to John Hingeston, keeper of the keyboard and wind instruments, and the other two are to provide him with clothing and money after his voice changed and he had officially 'gone from the Chapel', though in reality he must have continued to work and learn in the same circles (fig.1). Knowing that Henry was brought up in the Chapel Royal we can make an informed guess about his early education. Warrants survive to show that music paper, pens and ink were provided for the choristers to be taught at least the rudiments of music, and that they received instruction in playing instruments: in 1669, for example, the Master of the Children, Henry Cooke, received £192 12s 'for learning the children on the violin, lute, theorbo and organ'. Payments were also made for teaching the boys Latin and writing.

In 1672 Cooke was succeeded by Pelham Humfrey, an ambitious young composer whom King Charles had sent to France and Italy to study. Perhaps the earliest music manuscript we have in Purcell's hand is his copy of Humfrey's anthem 'By the waters of Babylon'. Like other anthems composed during the reign of Charles II for the principal services of the Chapel Royal, 'By the waters' has a string introduction and interludes, which in this copy Purcell has truncated and arranged somewhat incompetently for the organ (fig.2). The form of the treble clef seen in the organ right-hand part is very uncommon in Purcell's copying, and the awkwardness of the organ arrangement seems to reflect an untrained talent: nevertheless, the text of the vocal sections is extremely accurate and provides a primary source of this fine work, the only one possibly copied during Humfrey's lifetime or even under his supervision.

Humfrey, who died at the age of 27 in 1674, had little opportunity to contribute to the next stage of Purcell's training, but his successor John Blow (1648-1707) was to be a vital formative influence and a colleague with whom Purcell seems to have exchanged ideas throughout his life (fig.3). Blow's monument in Westminster Abbey states that he had been 'master to the late famous Mr Henry Purcell' and Henry Hall suggests that both he and Purcell had studied with the older composer:

R. White ad Vivum   delin. et sculpsit.

Dr John Blow.

4. Part of Blow's 'Rules for playing of a Through Bass upon Organ & Harpsicon'. (BL Add. MS.34072 f.2r)

Apollo's harp at once our souls did strike,
We learnt together, but not learnt alike:
Though equal care our master might bestow,
Yet only Purcell e'er shall equal Blow.

The two youths may have learnt together from Blow's brief but useful keyboard harmony handbook (fig.4). By the 1670s all accompanists, whether playing keyboards or other chordal instruments such as the theorbo, were expected to be able to supply appropriate chords over a figured or unfigured bass or from a treble-and-bass outline, and figured bass notation was commonly used as a shorthand, as a means of teaching harmony and as a medium for discussing the theory of music. The Blow handbook is not in his own writing and may well have been copied out by one of his pupils.

An important early Blow autograph (Christ Church, Oxford, MS Mus 628) suggests that he took an unusual pride and interest in Purcell's work. Beautifully copied, this

score contains Chapel Royal anthems by Pelham Humfrey and Blow himself, and a number of sacred partsongs by Purcell: some of the Blow anthems are thought to have been composed by 1677, and it is likely that Christ Church 628 contains what Blow saw as the finest music of his predecessor Pelham Humfrey, his own latest compositions and work in a different genre by his talented pupil. Further evidence of a relationship between pupil and teacher developing into a partnership of colleagues can be found in other manuscripts, such as an organ part of Blow's anthem 'God is our hope and strength' only recently recognized as Purcell's handwriting (fig. 5). The untidiness of the copy, and the fact that by failing to fit the music onto one side of the sheet Purcell rendered the part unusable in performance (and thereby probably ensured its survival), indicate that he was arranging it from an open score rather than copying from an existing organ part. Blow was awarded a Lambeth doctorate in December 1677, so the ascription of this work to 'Mr' Blow suggests that it was copied before that date.

5. John Blow, 'God is our hope and strength': organ part arranged by Purcell before the end of 1677. (Christ Church, Oxford, MS Mus 554 f.3r)

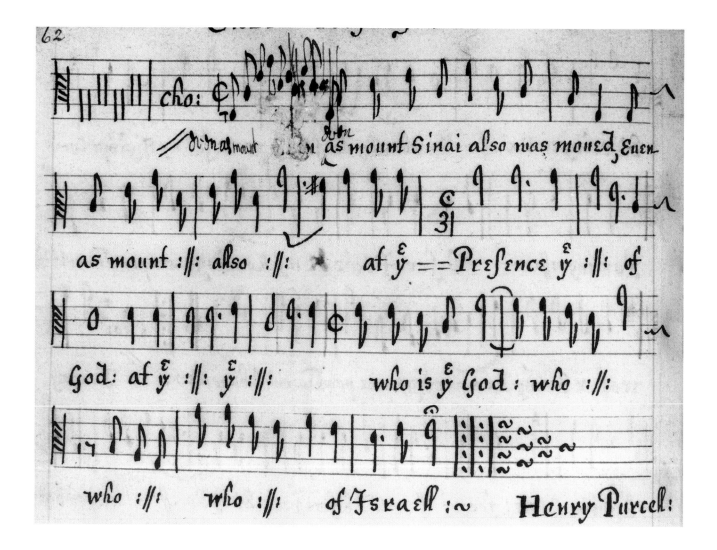

There is no doubt that by 1676 or 1677 Purcell was writing ambitious music of his own for Westminster Abbey and the Chapel Royal. The Abbey owns an incomplete set of partbooks containing Purcell anthems copied by William Tucker (d.1679), who makes ascriptions to 'Mr' Blow and was paid for copying anthems, presumably the extant set, in 1677. One part of Purcell's 'Let God arise' has alterations that appear to be in the composer's own writing (fig.6). Another Tucker copy dating from no later than 1677, this time of anthems with strings for the Chapel Royal, is the bass part-book BL Add. MS.50860, which includes Purcell's 'My beloved spake' and other works as well as two of the Blow anthems found in Christ Church 628: an autograph of 'My beloved spake' bound in BL Add. MS.30932 shows that the version Tucker copied was not the original, though of course Purcell could have proceeded from his draft to his final version in a very short time. In contrasting mood, Purcell's first autograph of his funeral sentences, in BL Add. MS.30931, seems from the somewhat awkward formation of the hand to be very early and may even have been made for Pelham Humfrey's funeral in 1674.

A third individual who had official charge of Purcell's training was John Hingeston,

‘keeper, maker, mender, repairer and tuner of the regals, organs, virginals, flutes and recorders and all other kinds of wind instruments whatsoever', whose assistant Purcell was appointed in 1673 (fig.7). Purcell must have made rapid progress, because from 1675 he was entrusted with the tuning of the organ in Westminster Abbey. He must also have looked after the John Player virginals belonging to the Palace of Whitehall, if not as an apprentice then after he succeeded to Hingeston's post in 1683 (Plate IX).

Hingeston's will (PRO PROB 11/375 ff.134r-135r) tells us that he was Purcell's godfather, confirms that Purcell's mother was called Elizabeth, the name of the wife of the elder Henry, and shows that Hingeston's collection of instruments included a ‘chest of viols', a complete set of five or six of these instruments including the then obsolete treble and tenor sizes. An interesting aspect of Purcell's development as a composer is his exploration of the old-fashioned fantazia form, a kind of polyphonic consort music almost exclusively for viols that had flourished in the first part of the seventeenth century. It is often said that Purcell wrote his fantazias purely as abstract exercises but one extant set of performing parts dating from around 1680 contains a three-part fantazia by Purcell (fig.8). The collection otherwise consists of music by

OPPOSITE TOP
6. A section of Purcell's ‘Let God arise': copied by William Tucker before the end of 1677 with autograph alterations. (Westminster Abbey, Triforium Set I, contratenor cantoris book f.58v)

OPPOSITE BOTTOM
7. John Hingeston (Faculty of Music, Oxford. Photograph: Bodleian Library, Oxford)

ABOVE
8. A copy of the second treble part of one of Purcell's 3-part fantazias, c.1680. The version here differs from that in his autograph. (BL Add. MS.31435 f.34v)

9. Matthew Locke (Faculty of Music, Oxford. Photograph: Bodleian Library, Oxford)

Matthew Locke (fig.9), the last major composer before Purcell to write in the fantazia form, and Christopher Gibbons, while inscriptions such as 'All the Fanta[zias] in this book of Mr Locks Exa[mined] by Mr Purcells Score Book' seem to refer to Locke's great autograph score BL Add. MS.17801. One of Purcell's earliest songs, 'What hope for us remains now he is gone?', is an elegy for Locke, whom Purcell succeeded as Composer for the Violins in September 1677. Christopher Gibbons, a famous keyboard player, was the son of Orlando Gibbons: he is sometimes identified as another of Purcell's teachers but none of his music, unlike that of Locke and Blow, survives in Purcell's hand.

Purcell's interest was not confined to music by composers he had known personally, and some of his consort music suggests that he had looked back well beyond Matthew Locke for his examples. In this respect Purcell's interest in the past was unusual, but in the realm of church music a small but important early repertory survived in general circulation, largely through the medium of John Barnard's intensely traditional *The First Book of Selected Church Musick* of 1641 which was acquired by several cathedrals after the Restoration. Neither the musical text nor the verbal underlay of Barnard's collection is completely satisfactory, and some of Purcell's copies of music by Elizabethan and Jacobean composers in Fitzwilliam Museum, Cambridge, MU MS 88 prove to be edited versions of Barnard texts. In Byrd's 'O Lord make thy servant', for example (fig.10), Purcell not only completes the underlay and modernizes the barring (compare the barring even in a recent work such as 'God is our hope and strength') but also corrects a passage where Barnard omitted a second tenor part which for several bars provides the bass. One wonders how long the expert choirs of the Chapel Royal or Westminster Abbey performed the work with an essential part missing before someone decided to find out what was wrong with it.

Fitzwilliam 88 is the earliest of the three great scorebooks that form Purcell's main autograph sources. This manuscript has undergone a considerable re-evaluation in recent years: its purpose is now considered to be at least as much concerned with the editing and preservation of the repertory it contains as with a process of self-education on Purcell's part, and the hand of the earliest part of the score, once thought to be Purcell's own immature writing, is accepted as the work of another copyist. In all probability Fitzwilliam 88 was a semi-official archival and rehearsal copy of some of the Chapel Royal repertory, including anthems both with and without strings.

The music copied by the first custodian of the book was indexed on 13 September 1677, and Purcell may have taken over shortly afterwards. The most likely candidate to be the earlier copyist is John Blow himself, who as a court composer and Master of the Children would have had good reason to make fair copies of the modern music that appears in the 1677 index. Both the text and music hands show striking similarities to early examples of Blow's copying, especially the calligraphic Christ Church 628, and an elaborate pen flourish on the final flyleaf could be read as 'JB'. The ascription of one anthem in the earlier hand to 'Mr Jo: Blow' is sometimes cited as proof that Blow himself cannot have been the copyist, but the score's formal purpose might have led him to make a formal self-ascription.

Purcell's contributions to the manuscript began at the reverse end, probably in or after December 1677 as all ascriptions to Blow refer to his doctorate though the first anthem at the reverse end of the book, Blow's 'O Lord, I have sinned', has no

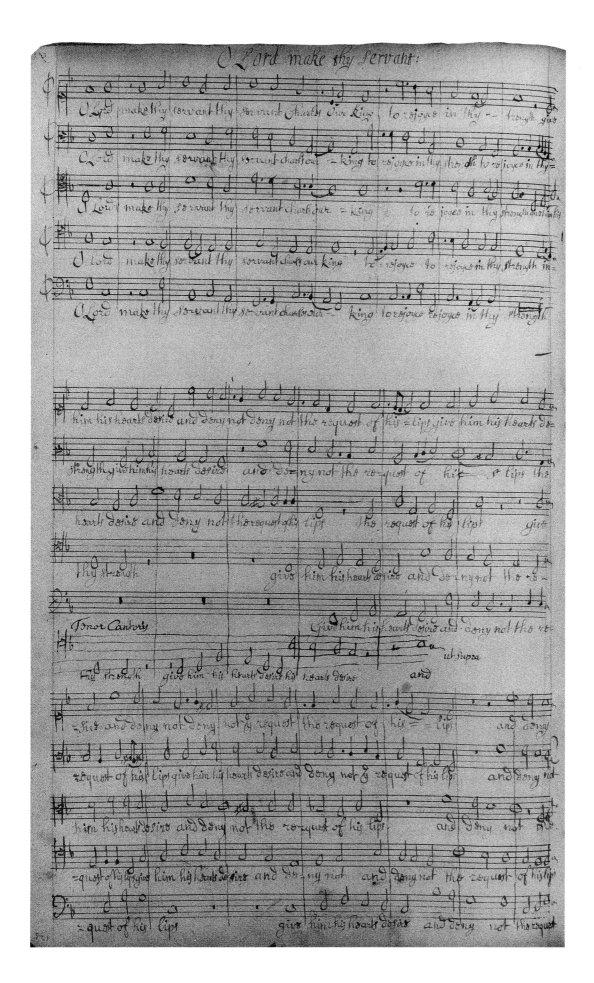

O Lord make thy Servant:

11. 'Jehova quam multi sunt hostes', a Latin sacred partsong by Purcell illustrating his writing c.1680. (BL Add. MS.30930 f.8v)

ascription at all. Significant changes in the handwriting suggest that Purcell continued to make additions to the book for some years, up to and after his writing of the inscription 'God bless Mr Henry Purcell', dated 10 September 1682, on the final flyleaf. Purcell's early handwriting has two particularly distinctive features: a reversed, hook-shaped bass clef, present in his Blow organ part but no longer regularly used by the time he started the Fitzwilliam manuscript, and a secretary hand 'e' in the text, replaced by an italic form by 1680. Purcell's writing style in or around 1680 can be seen in his autograph copy of 'Jehova quam multi sunt hostes' (fig.11), and we are probably justified in assigning dates before 1678 to copies consistently using both the early bass clef and secretary 'e', though how long before is a matter of estimation; those combining the modern bass clef with the older 'e' seem to belong to the years 1678-80. Further alterations take place between 1682 and 1685.

The Purcell sacred partsongs copied by Blow in Christ Church 628 were written out again by Purcell himself in BL Add. MS.30930, dated 1680 on its title page and elsewhere. The structure of this volume suggests that Purcell worked for some time on unbound sheets, and the manuscript's contents, which also include the fantazias and some of the sonatas, are mostly domestic chamber music, so Add. MS.30930 was prob-

Henry Purcell Gent.ⁿ
of his Chappell.

These are to certifie all whom it may concerne that by vertue of a Warrant from the R.^t Reverend Father in God Henry Lord B.^p of London and Deane of his Matie Chappell Royalle bearing date the 14.th July 1682 and in the 34.th year of his Matie Reigne; I have sworne and admitted Henry Purcell A Gentleman of his Matie Chappell Royalle in Ordinary in the place of Edward Lowe dec.^d To have and enjoy all Wages, Fees, Rights, priviledges, and proffitts thereto belonging.

Let this Certificate be entred this 21.th Xber 1683.

Wm Holder Sub-Dean.

Ste. Fox.

ably a private rather than an official copy: its apparently unbound origin could mean that music for which no autograph score survives, such as the sonatas published in 1683, was copied on further quires of the same stock of paper.

The choice of an event or date with which to conclude the first phase of Purcell's career is largely arbitrary. He was probably regarded by his colleagues as a fully-fledged composer in the late 1670s and by his 21st birthday he already held appointments at court and as organist of Westminster Abbey. The year of his marriage to Frances Peters, 1682, should not be regarded as the end of his apprenticeship, but perhaps as the beginning of a second stage of his adult career after his appointment as an organist of the Chapel Royal, in succession to Edward Lowe (fig. 12).

12. 'A Booke for the Entring of Certificates for the Chamber, Chappell and Stables 1682': certificate of Purcell's admission as a Gentleman of the Chapel Royal in place of Edward Lowe, who had been one of the three organists. (PRO LS13/197 f.91v)

The Glory of the Temple: 1682-88

Between 1682 and 1688 Purcell's musical life, including his composing, continued to be centred on Whitehall (Plate 11). Major works of this period include a series of Chapel Royal verse anthems with strings: for the secular ceremonial of the court he provided a sequence of welcome songs performed to greet the monarch on his return to Whitehall after his annual summer progress and occasional works such as a wedding ode for Princess Anne and Prince George of Denmark, all large-scale compositions for soloists, chorus, and an orchestra sometimes including woodwind instruments.

The principal musical document of Purcell's work in these years is the third and last of his great autograph scores, BL Music Library MS. R.M.20.h.8. With the exception of an anthem by Blow and a sacred song by Maurizio Cazzati this manuscript is devoted entirely to music by Purcell, and is mainly in his own hand: the most important of his three assistants was a prolific if somewhat inaccurate copyist who later transcribed BL Add. MS.31449, one of the principal sources of *The Indian Queen*.

In R.M.20.h.8. Purcell copied anthems from one end and secular works from the other, beginning with 'Swifter Isis', the welcome song for 1681. Between the welcome songs he included other vocal music ranging from solo songs to ensemble compositions with instruments, so the manuscript could be described as a 'Whitehall book' in which Purcell kept copies of all the music he might need around the palace for services in the Chapel Royal, formal occasions, or private entertainment in the King's apartments. The chronological layout of the secular music section of the manuscript not only enables us to date the works that lie between the welcome songs but also provides a further guide to the development of Purcell's writing, the main feature of which is the gradual replacement between 1682 and 1685 of the old secretary form of the letter 'r' in the text with a more modern italic version.

During the 1680s an attempt was apparently made to collect the entire secular court repertory of the Restoration period, including 'Swifter Isis', in an unusually splendid manuscript score (fig.13). 'Isis' is another name for the River Thames, and this welcome song was probably composed for the King's return, by river, from Windsor on 27 August 1681: in passing, it serves as a reminder of the river's importance as a thoroughfare within London and Westminster and as a means of reaching outlying places. In Purcell's time, the river was still the city's axis (fig.14).

As well as the major autograph R.M.20.h.8. a number of other manuscripts in Purcell's hand survive from this period. Some, like the anthem 'I was glad' in Birmingham University Barber Institute MS 5001, are evidently rough copies, perhaps even first drafts, of works later transcribed into the fair-copy score. Another manuscript of this period is a hastily-written score of the anthem 'Lord thou art become gracious' by Daniel Roseingrave (fig.15), the music in Purcell's hand but the text incipits in Roseingrave's: probably the composer, then organist of Winchester Cathedral, had lost his own copy of this work and asked Purcell to copy one for him in London, later adding the text incipits himself.

The last anthem in R.M.20.h.8. copied in Purcell's own hand rather than that of an assistant is the magnificent 'My heart is inditing', composed for the coronation of James II though the anthem actually belongs to the Queen's part of the ceremony.

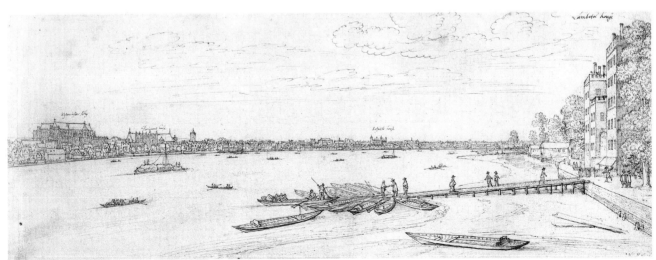

15. A rough copy by Purcell of an anthem by Daniel Roseingrave, *c.*1682: the title and text incipits are in Roseingrave's own hand. (Christ Church, Oxford, MS Mus 1215)

James's second wife Mary of Modena (Plate IV) led an unfortunate life: a foreigner and a Catholic, she was deeply unpopular on her first arrival in England in 1673 (fig.16) and the object of all kinds of vicious rumour, though by the time of the coronation the dignity of her conduct had at least earned the respect of the diarist John Evelyn. She left her mark on English music in several ways: apart from Purcell's coronation anthem, her marriage to James was celebrated by a performance at Drury Lane of a French opera, *Ariane, ou le mariage de Bacchus*, and when, after a series of miscarriages, she seemed in early 1688 to be safely pregnant Purcell composed the anthem 'Blessed are they that fear the Lord' for 'the Thanksgiving appointed to be in London & 12 miles round Jan 15 1687 [old style] & on the 29th following over England for the Queen's being with Child'. The birth on 10 June of her son James, a Catholic heir to the throne, helped to precipitate the revolution at the end of the year and the resultant exile of James II and his family.

Purcell's coronation anthem is laid out on the grandest scale. Its eight-part chorus and four-part string orchestra require a twelve stave system, so that even in so large

A Perspective of WESTMINSTER-ABBY from the High-Altar to the West end, shewing the manner of His Majesties CROWNING.

W. Sherwin sculp.

a volume as R.M.20.h.8. there is, in the choruses, room for only one system on a page: in such sections Purcell joins the staves on facing pages together and copies across complete openings (Plate III). The unusual layout of the vocal parts, with different clefs for each of the two treble parts and three rather than two basses, is also found in the preceding anthem in the coronation, Blow's 'God spake sometimes in visions', and reflects the composers' awareness of the voices available to them on this exceptional occasion.

Through the detailed illustrated account of the coronation published by Francis Sandford in 1687 we know a great deal about the performance of 'My heart is inditing'. The musicians occupied three galleries separated by some distance (fig.17): Sandford's plan of the Abbey shows that the singers in the gallery on the left belonged to the Chapel Royal, and that they were supported by a small organ, provided for the purpose by Purcell in his capacity of Keeper of the Organs. Opposite them were 'The King's quire of Instrumentall Musick' and in the distance, beyond the transept but on the same side as the instrumentalists, the Abbey choir, presumably accompanied by the Abbey's organ. A white-robed figure amongst the Chapel Royal singers appears to be conducting the whole performance with a baton, while the gentleman next to him seems to be relaying the beat to the rest of his choir: in the distance, the Abbey singers are holding their books up and have their eyes on the conductor in exemplary fashion.

As far as the choirs are concerned the artist appears to represent the performance very much as one would expect. In the instrumentalists' gallery, however, the players seem impossibly crowded, no music is in evidence, and a double courtal and a sackbut are being played. Other engravings show these instruments amongst the choirs during the procession to the abbey, so it is possible that knowing they had been taken into the building the artist felt he ought to show them somewhere: if they were played inside, it would probably have been to reinforce the Chapel Royal's little organ rather than with the instrumental group, who took their places before the service and did not walk in the procession. Another view shows what looks like a large plucked instrument, such as a theorbo, amongst the instrumentalists, and something of the sort might well have been used to play the continuo part. The view shown in fig.17 clearly indulges in a degree of artistic licence, because it depicts the performance of an anthem during the crowning of the King when, Sandford tells us, no anthem was actually sung but 'the trumpets [visible in the west gallery] sounded a Point of War, the Drums (which were without) Beat a Charge, and the People with loud and repeated Shouts cried GOD SAVE THE KING'.

What remains a mystery is why, as far as the score reveals, Purcell attempted neither to exploit the spatial possibilities of the situation nor to mitigate the problems the distance between the performers would undoubtedly cause. A contemporary dictionary, Edward Philips's *The New World of Words* of 1696, gives as part of the definition of an anthem that it should consist 'of Verses sung alternatively by the two opposite Quires, and Chorus's' so it seems likely that although the score does not give such indications the solo verses in this work were taken either by one choir or the other. Some of the chorus passages would also have been very difficult to co-ordinate across such a distance, and a possible explanation is that in places the two full choirs alternated not for brief echo effects but as part of the large-scale structure of the work. Choruses that seem to demand the combined strength of both choirs, such as 'With joy and gladness' at least begin in a rhythmically straightforward manner and are punctuated by string interludes that would help the choirs to make clean, unanimous starts.

Once the excitement of the coronation was over, the new King's rule had serious consequences for the court musicians. The Anglican Chapel Royal did not enjoy its previous status under an openly Catholic monarch, and before long the setting up of a Catholic Chapel Royal partly staffed by foreign singers might have caused some irritation; despite James's attempts to improve court administration the musicians' traditional difficulty in getting paid apparently continued. Nevertheless, James does seem to have been interested in his court music and Purcell continued to copy secular works into R.M.20.h.8. for most of his reign: a surviving copy of Purcell's bill for various outstanding payments during this period includes those due for numerous rehearsals of court odes, and suggests that a high standard of performance was still expected and appreciated (PRO T27/11 p.314).

After the Glorious Revolution: church, court and chamber music, 1689-95

It is impossible to know whether Purcell regarded the events of 1688 with relief, dismay or indifference, although the vulnerability of court musicians to the religious or political attitudes of their masters suggests that such service was not for those of an anxious disposition. After the coronation of William III and Mary II in 1689 the court was no longer the important musical centre it had been before, although Queen Mary (Plate v) was undoubtedly fond of music and Purcell's odes to celebrate her birthday are amongst his finest works. The regular performance of elaborate anthems in the Chapel Royal was not resumed under the new Protestant monarchs, and William's protracted absences on foreign campaigns together with his dislike of London meant that there was less for the court musicians to do.

One anthem performance in William's reign has nevertheless left some fascinating evidence. In 1690 William undertook what was for him a successful campaign against James's forces in Ireland (fig.19), and his return to England was marked by a celebration at Windsor on 9 September (fig.20). A score of Purcell's anthem 'My song shall be alway' copied by Francis Withey of Oxford bears the same date, which suggests not only that the anthem was performed on that occasion but also that Oxford musicians were recruited to take part in it (fig.21), and a set of instrumental parts, the only such contemporary material existing for any anthem by Purcell and partly in his own hand, survives at Christ Church, Oxford (fig.22). The work's special significance for Oxford musicians is underlined by the splendid score, BL Add. MS.17840, written by a copyist known to have been employed at Christ Church in the 1690s.

As well as odes to celebrate the Queen's birthday, Purcell had also in 1695 to compose a similar work for the sixth birthday of William, Duke of Gloucester, the only

18. Robert White: William, Duke of Gloucester. (British Museum Prints and Drawings Department)

surviving son of Princess Anne and Prince George. A weak and sickly child who did not survive to adulthood, William had a passion for military things which Purcell perhaps indulged through his trumpet writing in the ode, although he was in any case tending to use trumpets in celebratory music during this period (figs 18 and 23).

It is probably a sign of Purcell's increasingly varied professional life that whereas the large scorebooks of the earlier part of his career collect his works in a systematic way, and seem to have a partly archival purpose, the two bound volumes from his later years are of a completely different character. Both the Gresham songbook and the British Library's newly-acquired keyboard manuscript are meant for practical every-day use, and are in a quarto format more easily manageable than the large folio of the earlier volumes. The Gresham autograph contains a wide repertory of songs, almost all for solo soprano and mostly drawn from theatre works or odes of the 1690s (fig. 24). The bass line of some songs is incomplete or absent, so Purcell may have compiled the book for a singer to learn from and for himself to use to accompany, harmonizing when necessary from the treble part, for informal concerts at court or elsewhere.

For the funeral of Queen Mary in March 1695 Purcell composed some of the music for which he is most widely known. Two eighteenth-century sources of his final setting of 'Thou knowest Lord', the sixth of the Anglican funeral sentences, fit it into a much earlier funeral setting by Thomas Morley, the restrained style of which it matches

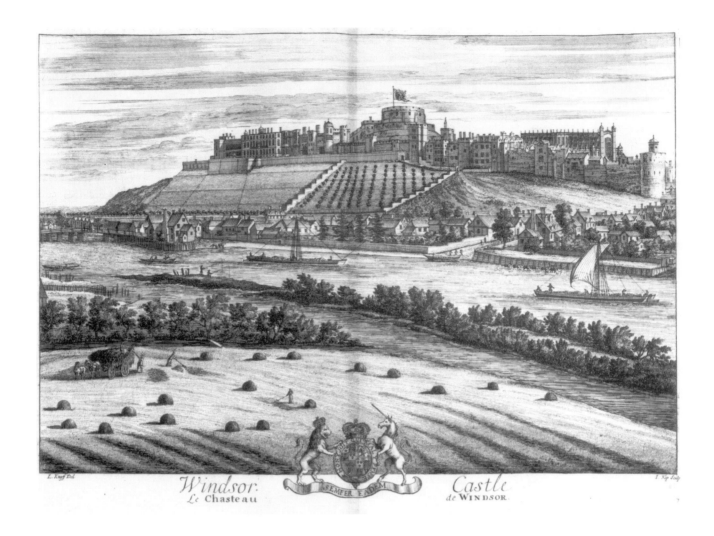

Windsor: *Le* Chasteau   SEMPER EADEM   Castle *de* WINDSOR.

admirably, and it is likely that out of respect for tradition Morley's music, with a single sentence composed by Purcell, was sung at the Queen's funeral. A score of 'Thou knowest Lord' copied by Thomas Tudway tells us that it was accompanied by 'flat Mournfull Trumpets' (fig. 25) and was performed again at Purcell's own burial. For the Queen's funeral Purcell also composed a march and canzona, to be played by the same 'flat trumpets' that accompanied 'Thou knowest Lord': these were trumpets fitted with slides to enable them to play a wider variety of notes, and the principal source, Oriel College, Oxford, MS U.a.37, states that the march was 'sounded before her [the Queen's] chariot'. Illustrations of the state funeral of the Duke of Albemarle in 1670 show not only the chariot bearing his effigy (fig. 26) but also trumpets being played ahead of it, though not slide trumpets, which are said to be very difficult to play on the move. The Oriel copyist, however, was responsible for several presentation manuscripts of music by Henry and Daniel Purcell and in the score of Daniel's 1700 Birthday Song for Princess Anne (BL Add. MS. 30934 ff. 36r-57v) takes over part of the copying from the composer. This musician was evidently close to the Purcell family, and his comment on the performance of the march is unlikely to be wrong.

ABOVE
21. Purcell, 'My song shall be alway' copied by Francis Withey and dated 9 September 1690. (Bodleian Library, Oxford, MS Mus. Sch. C.61 f.73r (inverted))

OPPOSITE
22. The second violin part of 'My song shall be alway', showing Purcell taking over from another copyist. (Christ Church, Oxford, MS Mus 1188-9 f.45r)

RIGHT
23. 'Who can from joy refrain?' (July 1695): Purcell's ode for the Duke of Gloucester's birthday. (BL Add. MS.30934 f.82v)

26

24. 'Strike the Viol': a transposed version, in Purcell's autograph, of a song from the 1694 birthday ode 'Come ye sons of art away'. (Guildhall Library, London: Gresham autograph)

28

touch touch touch touch touch ye Lute Wake ye Harp

ye Flute Wake ye Harp inspire ye Flute   Flute

yo Patroneses praise sing sing sing in chear

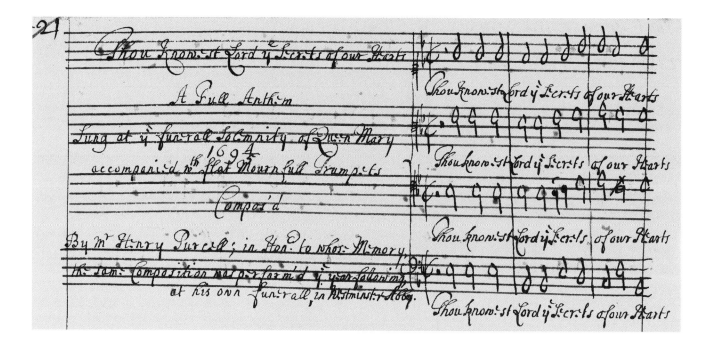

TOP

25. 'Thou knowest Lord the secrets of our hearts': Purcell's final setting copied and annotated by Thomas Tudway. (BL Harl. 7340 f.264v)

BOTTOM

26. The 'chariot' at a seventeenth-century state funeral: on this occasion the body had already been privately buried. Francis Sandford, *Solemn Interment* (BL 567.k.23. plate 18)

The Glory of the Stage:
music for the theatre

The London theatres of Purcell's boyhood years were run by two patent companies established at the Restoration, the King's Company led by Thomas Killigrew and the Duke's under Sir William Davenant. Some significant features of their productions, such as the performance of female parts by women instead of boys and the use of scenery, were derived from the indoor Court theatre and the pre-Commonwealth court masque rather than from the open-air tradition of the public playhouse, which had been suppressed during the Civil War and Commonwealth; a few entertainments with masque-like characteristics, such as James Shirley's *Cupid and Death* and Davenant's own *The Siege of Rhodes* (in which Purcell's father was one of the singers) had taken place during the 1650s and perhaps help to explain why Restoration theatre developed as it did.

The great majority of Restoration theatrical performances were straight plays, which nevertheless featured music between the acts and in places where songs, dances or other music could appropriately be brought in to the action. By the mid-1670s, however, both companies were working in specially-constructed theatres capable of mounting productions with elaborate scenic effects, the King's Company at Drury Lane and the Duke's at Dorset Garden, and the facilities of these buildings made possible performances in which spectacle and music, essential aspects of the earlier masque tradition, were much more prominent. Apparently miraculous changes of scene before the audiences' eyes, machinery to enable gods or demons to descend from the heavens or rise from the earth and extended passages of music were important elements of these performances, which sometimes took the form of self-contained masques set within spoken plays, such as the Act IV Masque of Orpheus and Eurydice in Elkanah Settle's *The Empress of Morocco* (1673); in other works, such as the adaption of *The Tempest* produced in 1674 or Shadwell's *Psyche* of 1675, music and spectacle assume so prominent a role that the drama can no longer be regarded as a play with incidental music. The term 'semi-opera' was later coined by Roger North to identify the new genre.

Historians of drama often regret our lack of detailed information about the two London theatres of Purcell's time, but we have far more evidence about them than, for example, the Chapel Royal or Purcell's domestic life. Their dimensions can be seen in contemporary large-scale maps: Dorset Garden in Ogilby and Morgan's map of 1677 (fig.27) and the King's in Drury Lane from Morgan's map of 1681/2. The overall length of Dorset Garden was less than 150 feet, and Drury Lane was even smaller. An engraving of the river façade of Dorset Garden was published in *The Empress of Morocco* in 1673, and the theatre's riverbank location, which would have made it easy for patrons to arrive by boat, is illustrated in the later of the two maps (fig.28). A good impression of the interior layout of a theatre is given by a sectional drawing made by Sir Christopher Wren, which may or may not be a working drawing for the 1674 rebuilding of Drury Lane but undoubtedly shows many essential features of the two theatres, such as the extension of the stage beyond the proscenium arch, sets of wings

27. Detail of Ogilby and
Morgan's map of 1677 showing
the Duke's Theatre (*ie* Dorset
Garden) by the river side.
(BL Map Library: C.7.b.4)

BELOW
28. Detail of Morgan's map of
1681/2, showing the river façade
of the Dorset Garden theatre
(BL Map Library: CRACE PORT.
II.58)

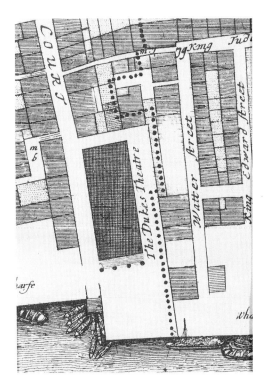

PLATE I (TOP)
Court musicians shortly after
the Restoration: traditionally
known as 'The Cabal' and
ascribed to J. B. Medina. (Nostell
Priory. Photograph: National
Trust Photographic Library/
Charlie Nickols)

PLATE II (BOTTOM)
Whitehall in the time of Charles II.
The banqueting house, on the
left, still stands. (Berkeley Castle)

PLATE IV
Mary of Modena, second wife of
James II, by William Wissing
(NPG no.214). By courtesy of the
National Portrait Gallery,
London.

PLATE V
Queen Mary II, after Wissing
(NPG no.606). By courtesy of the
National Portrait Gallery,
London.

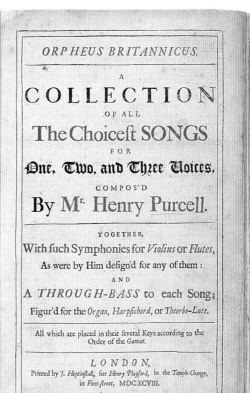

PLATE VIII
John Dryden: a portrait dated
1693 by Sir Godfrey Kneller.

Dryden wrote the text of
Purcell's *King Arthur* and the
elegy *Mark now the lark and linnet
sing* set to music by John Blow.
(NPG no.2083). By courtesy of
the National Portrait Gallery,
London.

Virginals built by John Player,
London 1664, and stamped
'WP' for Whitehall Palace.
(Cobbe collection of historical
keyboard instruments,
Hatchlands)

PLATE X
Henry Purcell, attributed to
John Closterman. (NPG no.4994).
By courtesy of the National
Portrait Gallery, London.

which could be used to change the scene, and a backward extension of the stage beyond the movable scenery to allow for perspective backdrops or 'relieves' (fig.29).

The two theatres of the 1670s may seem small by modern standards, but they were larger than the Whitehall theatres into which, before the Civil War, Inigo Jones had fitted stage sets with the same scenic elements. For the 1640 masque *Salmacida Spolia* he produced sectional and plan views of the scenery and machines showing four sets of wings, each with four interchangeable flats, and four shutters, which meet in the centre; behind the shutters is a backcloth and space to store perspective 'relieves'. Above the wings and shutters are two sets of 'borders' depicting the top of the scene,

29. A cross-sectional drawing of a theatre by Sir Christopher Wren, possibly a preliminary design for the 1674 rebuilding of the King's Theatre in Drury Lane. (All Souls' College, Oxford, II, 81)

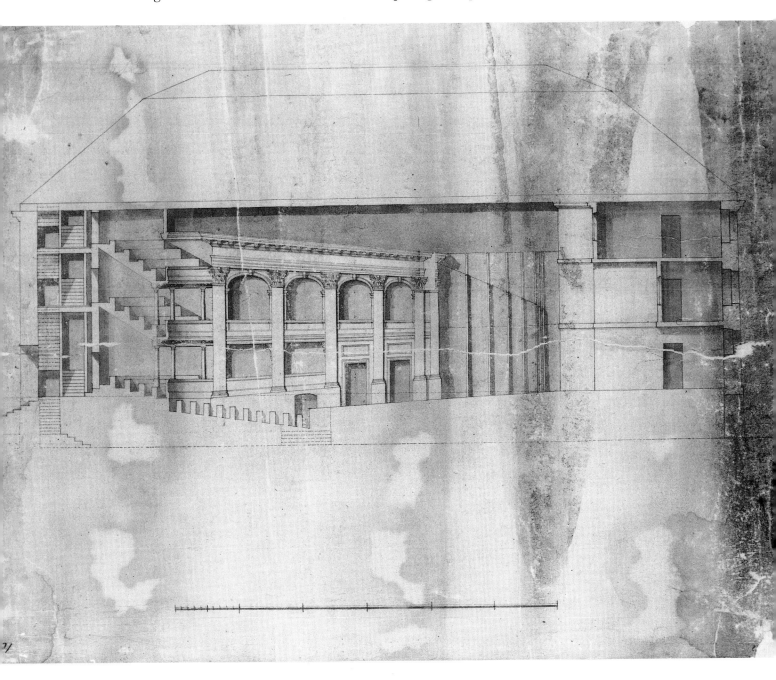

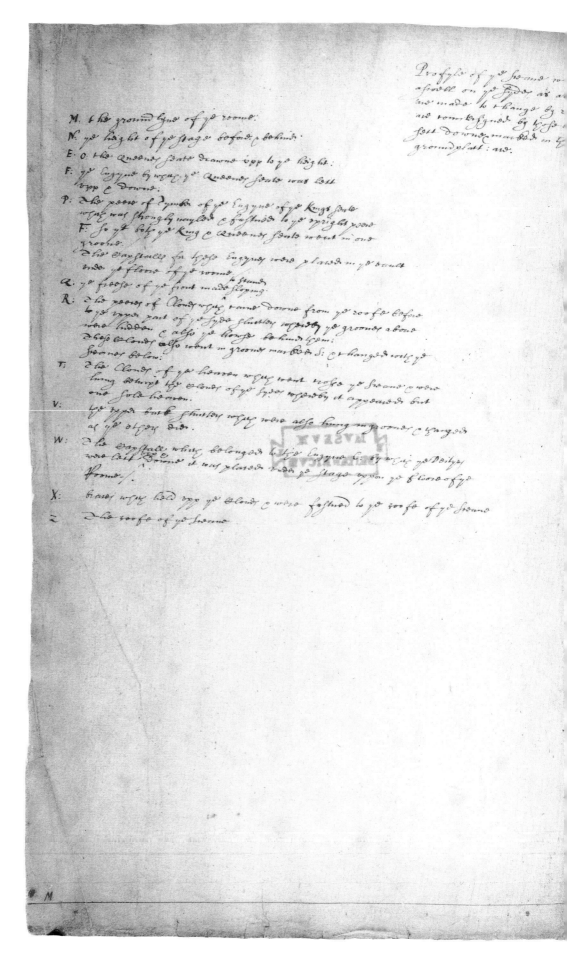

30. Inigo Jones: a cross-section of the scenery and mechanism for *Salmacida Spolia*, 1640. (BL Lansdowne 1171 ff.1v - 2r)

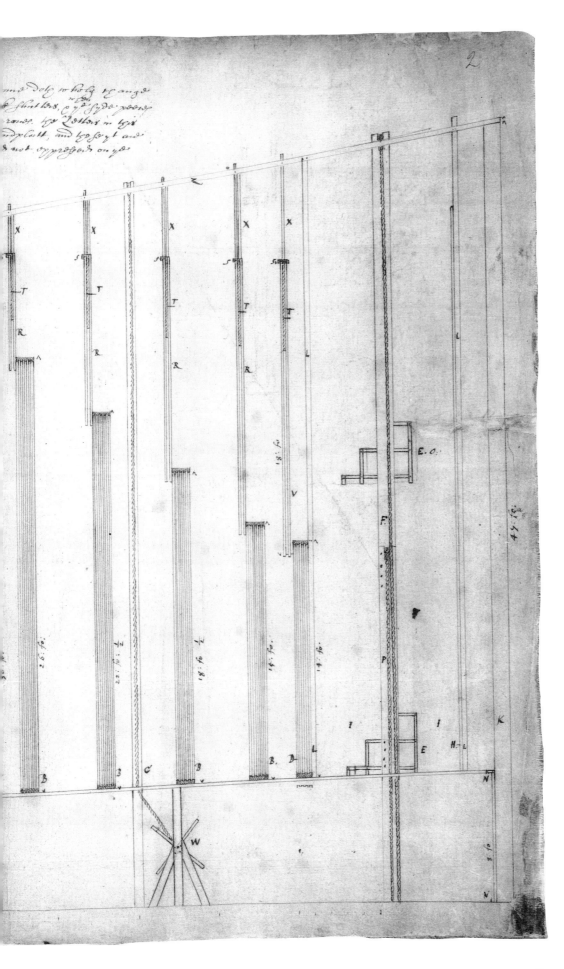

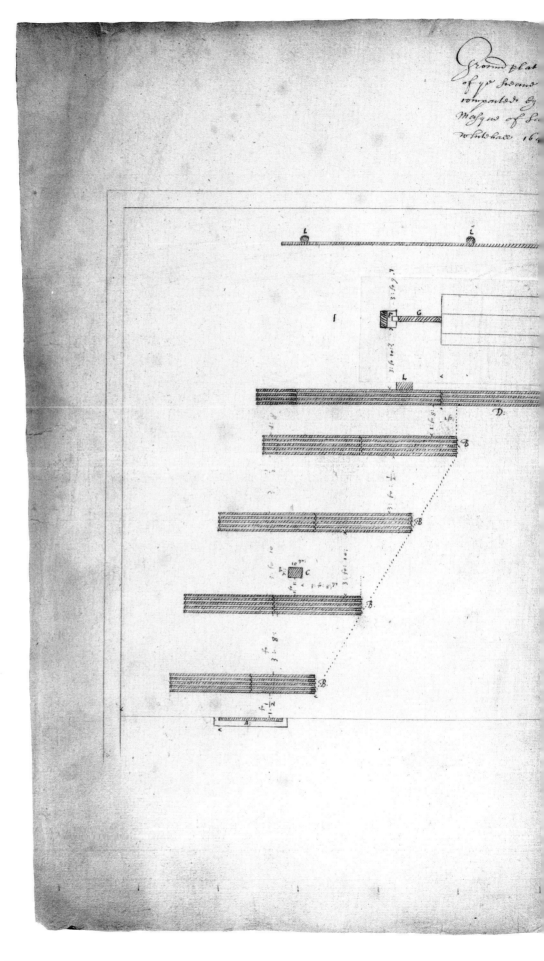

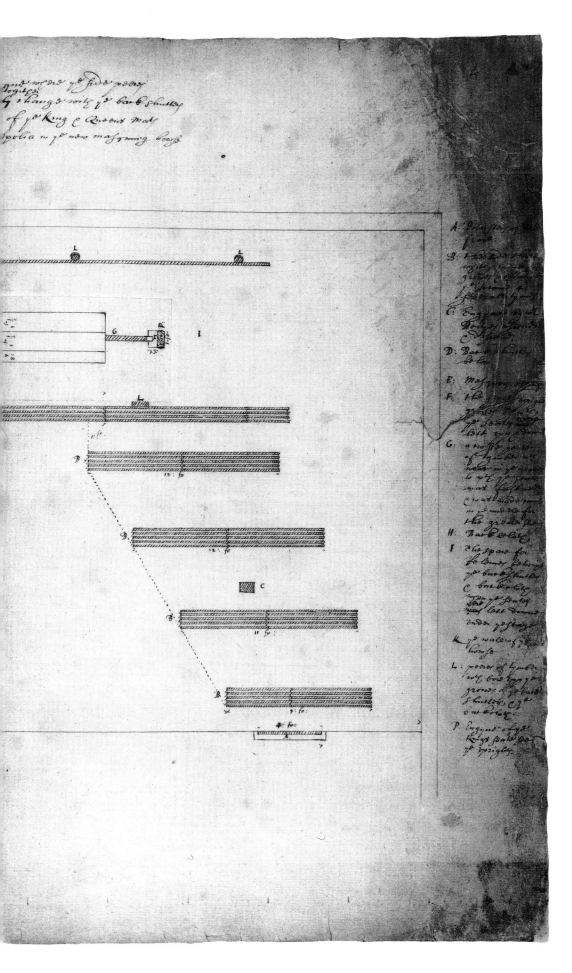

32. An engraving of a perspective set: Elkanah Settle, *The Empress of Morocco* (BL 644.i.8. plate facing p.1)

one apparently fixed and supporting the grooves for moving the other. Jones's section also shows one of the three capstans beneath the stage and two of the three seats in which characters were raised and lowered. All this was fitted into a stage measuring no more than 28 feet from proscenium to backcloth: the proscenium arch was about 35 feet wide and 30 feet high (figs 30 and 31).

The *Salmacida* drawings date from before Purcell's lifetime, but they are the most comprehensive English illustration of the scenic methods adopted by the Restoration theatres. The effect of the perspective stage is well illustrated by five engravings published in *The Empress of Morocco* (fig.32), and a Royal proclamation of 1674 'for keeping good order in the Playhouse' gives an indication of the effort involved in scene changes as well as an insight into the habits of contemporary playgoers (fig.33):

... 'tis impossible to command those vast Engines (which move the Scenes and Machines) and to order such a number of Persons as must be employed in Works of that nature, if any but such as belong thereunto, be suffered to press in amongst them.

Purcell can hardly have been unaware of the major musical productions of the 1670s. At the opening of the 1674 *Tempest*, performed at Dorset Garden, an elaborate scenic representation of a storm is underlined by Matthew Locke's famous 'Curtain Tune', with its rushing scales and then novel directions such as 'lowder by degrees' and 'violent': this work, and the music by Locke and Draghi in *Psyche* (1675), must have been known to Purcell and in due course have provided a model for his own dramatic music. Another semi-opera, *Circe*, with music by John Banister, was produced in 1677. At Drury Lane in 1674 a French opera company performed *Ariane, ou le mariage de Bacchus*, for which Louis Grabu, then Master of the King's Music, probably adapted earlier music by Robert Cambert: again, the frontispiece of the published libretto shows an impressive perspective set and the stage directions show that machinery and trapdoors were available. Works presented at court, such as the 1675 'Maske at Whitehall' *Calisto* with music by Nicholas Staggins, must also have contributed to Purcell's experience of dramatic music.

The patent companies combined in 1682 to form the United Company, which used the larger and better-equipped theatre at Dorset Garden for productions requiring elaborate scenery and Drury Lane for the less complicated spoken plays. All Purcell's major dramatic works were therefore produced at Dorset Garden, although he composed songs and incidental music for many plays performed at the smaller theatre.

Purcell composed some quite ambitious music for Lee's *Theodosius* in 1680, but otherwise, with the possible exception of *Dido and Aeneas*, which was not performed in a public theatre during his lifetime, most of his theatre music dates from after the Glorious Revolution. By this time Purcell could have built upon his experience of theatre music in the 1670s by acquiring an extensive knowledge of contemporary dramatic works. Instrumental suites derived from Lully's operas were certainly known in England by the 1680s and it is probable that printed scores of entire works were also available; Lully's *Cadmus et Hermione* may have been performed in London in 1686; in 1685 there was a production of Grabu's all-sung *Albion and Albanius*, a French opera in every respect except the language of its libretto by John Dryden (Plate VIII). The elaborate printed score of *Albanius*, resembling the editions in which Lully's works were published in Paris, provided a model for Purcell's own publication of *Dioclesian*.

Charles R.

WHereas Complaint hath often been made unto Us, That divers Persons do rudely press, and with evil Language and Blows force their way into Our Theatres, (called the Theatre Royal in Bridges-street, and the Dukes Theatre in Dorset-Garden) at the time of their Publick Representations and Actings, without paying the Price established at both the said Theatres, to the great disturbance of Our Servants, Licenced by Our Authority, as well as others, and to the danger of the Publick Peace: Our Will and Pleasure therefore is, and We do hereby straightly Charge and Command, That no Person of what Quality soever do presume to come into either of the said Theatres before and during the time of Acting, and until the Plays are quite finished, without paying the Price established for the respective Places. And Our further Command is, That the Money which shall be so paid by any Persons for their respective Places, shall not be return'd again, after it is once paid, notwithstanding that such Persons shall go out at any time before or during the Play; And (to avoid future Fraud) That none hereafter shall enter the Pit, First, or Upper Gallery, without delivering to the respective Door-keeper the Ticket or Tickets which they received for their Money paid at the first Door.

And forasmuch as 'tis impossible to command those vast Engines (which move the Scenes and Machines) and to order such a number of Persons as must be employed in Works of that nature, if any but such as belong thereunto, be suffer'd to press in amongst them; Our Will and Command is, That no Person of what Quality soever, presume to stand or sit on the Stage, or to come within any part of the Scenes, before the Play begins, while 'tis Acting, or after 'tis ended; and We strictly hereby Command Our Officers and Guard of Souldiers which attend the respective Theatres, to see this Order exactly observ'd. And if any Person whatsoever shall disobey this Our known Pleasure and Command, We shall proceed against them as Contemners of Our Royal Authority, and Disturbers of the Publick Peace.

Given at Our Court at *Whitehall* the Second day of *February* in the Twenty sixth Year of Our Reign.

LONDON,

Printed by the Assigns of *John Bill* and *Christopher Barker*, Printers to the Kings most Excellent Majesty. 1673.

40

Leaving aside *Dido and Aeneas*, Purcell's main dramatic works are the four semi-operas *Dioclesian* (1690), *King Arthur* (1691), *The Fairy Queen* (1692) and *The Indian Queen* (1695). All follow the example of earlier semi-operas in that music plays an essential part in the drama but does not articulate the basic plot. In the famous 'Frost Scene' in *King Arthur*, for example, Purcell's music helps to integrate and underline a scenic transformation and the ascent of the Cold Genius from the earth, a demonstration of magical power which is part of the evil Osmond's attempt to seduce the heroine Emmeline: the scene's relevance to the situation is evident, but Emmeline and Osmond do not sing at all, either here or elsewhere (figs 34 and 35). Other than the semi-operas, Purcell's large-scale theatre scores included a substantial masque in *Timon of Athens*, extended instrumental and vocal contributions to *Bonduca*, *Circe* and *The Libertine*, a number of songs for *Don Quixote* and the incantation scene in *Oedipus*, source of the famous song 'Music for a while'.

Purcell's last year was overshadowed by dissent in the theatre. Following a long period of worsening relationships between actors and management, most of the United Company's experienced performers seceded to form a new company, led by the influential Thomas Betterton, which soon began presenting plays at a re-opened theatre in Lincoln's Inn Fields. *The Indian Queen* was therefore performed by an inexperienced cast including very young singers such as the teenager Letitia Cross, and the boy treble Jemmy Bowen. Nor were Purcell's difficulties confined to casting: whether because of illness or for some other reason he was unable to finish the score and the concluding masque was composed by Daniel Purcell.

Between 1690 and 1695 composing music for the public theatres must have occupied Purcell as much as court and Chapel Royal music had ten years previously, but there is no theatrical equivalent to the great autograph scores of the earlier years. *Dioclesian* was published in 1690 and the partial autograph of *The Fairy Queen* (Royal Academy of Music, London, MS.3) was evidently prepared under his supervision for a forthcoming performance. Other manuscript sources of Purcell's semi-operas are less reliable: none of the sources of *King Arthur* contains a satisfactory version of the end of the work and the score of *The Indian Queen* in BL Add. MS.31449, almost certainly a theatre file copy as it contains the text as well as the music, is highly inaccurate although the music copyist was a long-standing assistant of Purcell.

The absence of authoritative source material for some of the semi-operas is regrettable but not surprising. Purcell made no second attempt at publishing the music of a semi-opera, no doubt because, as the publisher John Walsh stated in a preface to Daniel Purcell's *Judgement of Paris* (1702), *Dioclesian* 'found so small Encouragement in Print, as serv'd to stifle many other Intire Opera's, no less Excellent': there was clearly no widespread public demand for scores of complete theatre works, and no need for the composer to draw up a complete fair-copy score for the theatre itself when each performance might be slightly different from the one before. Individual songs and incidental music extracted from stage works of all kinds, however, gained a wide circulation through printed collections, single-sheet publications and manuscripts.

Dido and Aeneas, Purcell's one through-composed opera – his only opera in the modern sense – does not belong to the world of the commercial public theatre for which he composed his other stage music. *Dido* is clearly related to Blow's *Venus and Adonis*, 'A Masque for the Entertainment of the King', which was performed at

33. A Royal proclamation of 2 February 1674 encouraging good order in the theatres. (PRO LC7/3 f.1)

Matil. He strikes a Horrour through my Blood.

Emm. I Freeze, as if his impious Art had fix'd
My Feet to Earth.

Ofm. But Love shall thaw ye.
I'll show his force in Countries cak'd with Ice,
Where the pale Pole-Star in the North of Heav'n
Sits high, and on the frory Winter broods;
Yet there Love Reigns: For proof, this Magick Wand
Shall change the Mildness of sweet *Britains* Clime
To *Yzeland*, and the farthest *Thule's* Frost;
Where the proud God, disdaining Winters Bounds,
O'er-leaps the Fences of Eternal Snow,
And with his Warmth, supplies the distant Sun.

*Osmond strikes the Ground with his Wand: The Scene
changes to a Prospect of Winter in Frozen Countries.*

Cupid Descends.

Cup. sings. *What ho, thou Genius of the Clime, what ho!!*
Ly'st thou asleep beneath those Hills of Snow?
Stretch out thy Lazy Limbs; Awake, awake,
And Winter from thy Furry Mantle shake.

Genius Arises.

Genius. *What Power art thou, who from below,*
Hast made me Rise, unwillingly, and slow,
From Beds of Everlasting Snow!
See'st thou not how stiff, and wondrous old,
Far unfit to bear the bitter Cold,

II

34. Stage directions requiring a
scene change and the use of
machinery: the beginning of the
Frost Scene in Dryden's libretto
for *King Arthur*. (BL 11774.d.5.
p.31)

OPPOSITE
35. Purcell's music for the
beginning of the Frost Scene in
King Arthur. (BL Add. MS.31447
f.33r)

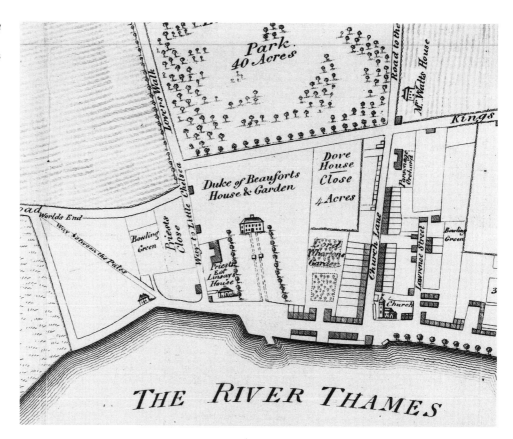

36. *Chelsea Surveyed in the Year 1664 by James Hamilton Continued to 1717:* detail locating Josias Priest's house. (Reprint of 1810 in *LCC Survey of London iv: The Parish of Chelsea* (London, 1913) Part II, plate 1)

37. The beginning of the libretto of *Dido and Aeneas.* (Royal College of Music 1.A.20)

OPPOSITE
38. Crispin de Passé, *Compendium Operum Virgilianorum* (Arnhem, 1612): an engraving compressing several episodes of the story of Dido and Aeneas (BL 78.b.20)

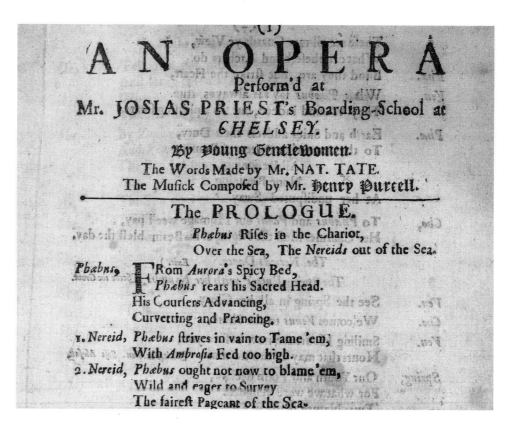

(1)

AN OPERA

Perform'd at

Mr. JOSIAS PRIEST's Boarding-School at
CHELSEY.

By Young Gentlewomen.

The Words Made by Mr. NAT. TATE.

The Musick Compos'd by Mr. Henry Purcell.

The PROLOGUE.

Phœbus Rises in the Chariot,
Over the Sea, The *Nereids* out of the Sea.

Phœbus. FRom *Aurora's* Spicy Bed,
Phœbus rears his Sacred Head.
His Coursers Advancing,
Curvetting and Prancing.

1. *Nereid,* *Phœbus* strives in vain to Tame 'em,
With *Ambrosia* Fed too high.

2. *Nereid,* *Phœbus* ought not now to blame 'em,
Wild and eager to Survey
The fairest Pageant of the Sea.

Whitehall in the early 1680s. The masque was later performed at Josias Priest's boarding school for young ladies at Chelsea (fig.36), an event less surprising than it might at first seem because Priest was a prominent choreographer deeply involved in the London theatre. Our only certain knowledge of the early history of *Dido* is that it too was performed at Priest's boarding school as the printed libretto states (fig.37) and, since a spoken epilogue by D'Urfey published in his *New Poems* of November 1689 apparently refers to the Glorious Revolution, the performance presumably took place in that year. There are, nevertheless, good reasons for suggesting that the opera might have been composed earlier, perhaps the most compelling of which is that *Dido*'s similarities of scale, form and subject matter with *Venus and Adonis* imply that the two works were conceived for a related purpose. The main sources of *Dido* date from well into the eighteenth century and cast no light on the work's origins.

The story of the opera is drawn from the fourth book of the Aeneid, available in the seventeenth century in translations such as Robert Howard's *The Loves of Dido and Aeneas*, where the central question is the culpability or otherwise of Dido's seduction of, rather than by, Aeneas. An illustrated French summary of the Aeneid published in 1612 gives an impression of the way seventeenth-century people would have imagined the ancient world and an indication of the effect a set designer might have aimed at (fig.38): the text that accompanies the pictures treats Dido's misfortune as entirely her own fault. Purcell and his librettist Nahum Tate make Dido rather than Aeneas the centre of the story and present her far more sympathetically: Purcell's success in dealing with a subject of such psychological complexity makes it a matter for regret that he never had occasion to write another completely sung opera.

Ardet amore gravi Dido, soror Annaĝ suadet
Nubere; at infausto sidere cæptus amor:
Nam postquam Æneas monity discedere, abyßet,
Ipsa sibi tristes attulit ægra manus.

Purcell and publishing

The dominant figure in English music publishing during the 1670s was John Playford (fig.39), who dealt in printed and manuscript music, as well as in blank manuscript books and paper, from a shop in the Inner Temple. He was succeeded in the mid-1680s by his son Henry. Although other publishers issued Purcell's music, not always in pirated editions, his clear preference was for the Playfords, with whom he seems to have been on terms of personal friendship: both John and Henry mention him in their wills, and he marked John's death with an elegy, 'Gentle shepherds, you that know'. John Playford's *Choice Ayres and Songs to Sing to the Theorbo-lute or Bass-viol ... the Second Book* of 1679 is the earliest publication to contain music undoubtedly by Purcell: four light hearted and sometimes cynical songs about love or drinking and, at the end of the volume, his elegy for Locke.

The Playfords normally used movable type for their editions, resorting to engraving only when there were compelling reasons to do so. John Playford employed a number of different printers, but all his typeset publications containing music by Purcell feature the Granjon typeface, which does not allow quavers or semiquavers to be beamed together as they would have been in manuscript music (see fig.45). Purcell preferred engraving for the 1683 edition of his sonatas (fig.40), apparently issued at his own risk although comparison between a page of the sonatas and a sample of John Playford's music hand suggests that the engraver, Thomas Cross, worked from an exemplar copied by Playford himself.

Superior typefaces became available from the late 1680s: the score of *Dioclesian* and other editions of the 1690s use the round-note Heptinstall typeface first introduced in 1687, which looks more attractive and allows short notes to be properly grouped (see fig.47). Another round-note type, which seems to have displaced Heptinstall's in 1699, was William Pearson's 'New London Character', employed in a number of eighteenth-century editions (fig.41). Engraving, though seldom used by the Playfords,

39. Francis Barlow: a drawing said to depict John Playford. This design, reversed, appears on the frontispiece of Playford's *Musick's Delight on the Cithren*, 1666 (British Museum Prints and Drawings Department)

OPPOSITE TOP
40. Engraving in a prestige edition: Purcell, *Sonnata's of III Parts* (1683): Violin II, p.1. (BL Music Library K.4.g.10)

OPPOSITE BOTTOM
41. A catch by Henry Aldrich printed in Pearson's 'New London Character': *The Second Book of the Pleasant Musical Companion* (1701) no.49. (BL Music Library A.412.e.). Purcell contributed about fifty catches to anthologies such as this.

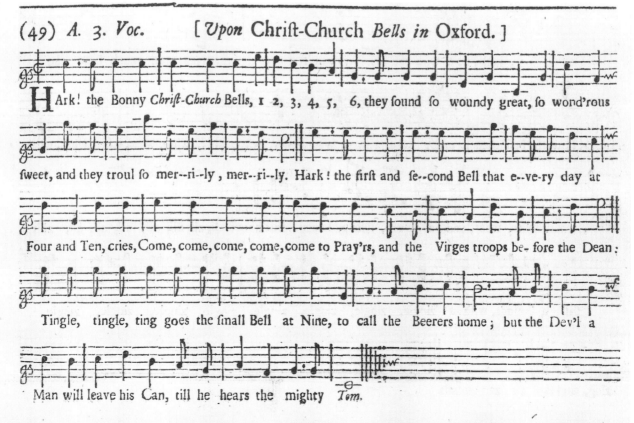

(49) *A. 3. Voc.*   [*Upon* Christ-Church *Bells in* Oxford.]

Hark! the Bonny *Christ-Church* Bells, 1 2, 3, 4, 5, 6, they found fo woundy great, fo wond'rous

fweet, and they troul fo mer--ri--ly, mer--ri--ly. Hark! the firft and fe--cond Bell that e--ve-ry day at

Four and Ten, cries, Come, come, come, come, come to Pray'rs, and the Virges troops be- fore the Dean:

Tingle, tingle, ting goes the fmall Bell at Nine, to call the Beerers home; but the Dev'l a

Man will leave his Can, till he hears the mighty *Tom.*

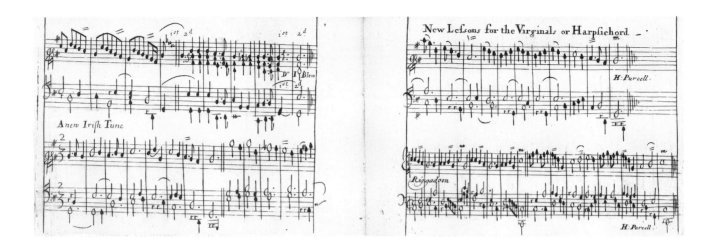

42. Engraved keyboard music:
Henry Playford, *The Second Part of
Musick's Handmaid ... carefully
Revised and Corrected by ... Mr
Henry Purcell*, 1689.
(BL Music Library K.4.b.10.(2))

was not confined to prestigious publications like the 1683 Purcell sonatas and was especially useful for keyboard music, as chords were difficult to set up in movable type (fig.42).

The majority of publications containing works by Purcell were anthologies, ranging from collections of often bawdy catches to Henry Playford's *Harmonia Sacra* volumes of 1688 and 1693, to which Purcell contributed some outstanding sacred songs as well as acting as the first book's editor. During his lifetime publications devoted exclusively to his own works were probably intended to advance his career as much as to make an immediate profit, but the same cannot be true of the posthumous publications *A Choice Collection of Lessons for the Harpsichord*, *A Collection of Ayres, Compos'd for the Theatre*, the sonatas of 1697, the Te Deum and *Orpheus Britannicus*. All but the last were published by Frances Purcell, and, as *Orpheus* contains a number of songs which had not been printed before, she probably obtained some payment from Henry Playford for these as well. Purcell's untimely death may well have led to a rush of publications that would otherwise have taken place more gradually, if at all, but his manuscripts must have been a great help to Frances in supporting herself and her young family, and the terms of his will, in which he bequeathed her 'all my Estate both reall and personall of what nature and kind soever', made sure that they were unequivocally hers to dispose of (PRO PROB 1/8).

Music for St Cecilia's Day

From 1683 until well into the eighteenth century a regular celebration of St Cecilia's Day took place in London on 22 November, or on the following day if the feast fell on a Sunday. The festivities, consisting of a church service followed by a banquet at which a newly-composed ode would be performed, were apparently promoted by the members of a 'Musical Society' who annually elected stewards to take charge of proceedings for the following year. The society's members comprised both professional musicians and gentleman amateurs, and admission seems to have been by ticket and by no means cheap (fig.43).

43. A ticket for a St Cecilia's Day celebration.

OVERLEAF LEFT
44. 'Welcome to all the pleasures', Purcell's 1683 St Cecilia's Day ode: title page. (BL Music Library к.4.c.18.)

OVERLEAF RIGHT
45. 'Welcome to all the pleasures'. The absence of a viola part suggests that the two violin parts printed are solos, the other instruments doubling the voices. (BL Music Library к.4.c.18. p.33)

The title page of Purcell's 1683 ode 'Welcome to all the pleasures' (fig.44), which provides the first definite evidence of the formal observation of St Cecilia's Day by London musicians, also implies that the practice was not completely new in 1683. The title page itself states that the saint's memory was 'annually honour'd by a public Feast made on that Day by the Masters and Lovers of Music, as well in England as in Foreign Parts' and there is nothing in the dedication to 'the Gentlemen of the Musical Society' to suggest that the celebration was new or unusual. Nevertheless, the only other contemporary Cecilian ode to have its music printed, Blow's 'Begin the song' of the very next year, is entitled *A Second Musical Entertainment perform'd on St Cecilia's Day*, so perhaps Purcell's 1683 ode was indeed the first. From 1684 the concert and banquet were held at Stationers' Hall, preceded by a service at St Bride's Church, for which, in 1694, Purcell composed his Te Deum and Jubilate in D.

In its overall length and organization 'Welcome to all the pleasures' broadly resembles Purcell's court odes of the same period, and employs a four-part string orchestra in the instrumental symphonies (fig.45). In 1687 Dryden's ode 'From

A
Musical Entertainment

PERFORM'D

On NOVEMBER XXII. 1683.

IT BEING THE

Festival of St. CECILIA, *a great Patroneſs of* Muſic;

WHOSE

MEMORY is ANNUALLY honour'd by a public *Feaſt*
made on that Day by the MASTERS and LOVERS of
Muſic, as well in *England* as in Foreign Parts.

LONDON,
Printed by *J. Playford* Junior, and are to be ſold by *John Playford* near the
Temple Church, and *John Carr* at the *Middle-Temple* Gate, 1684.

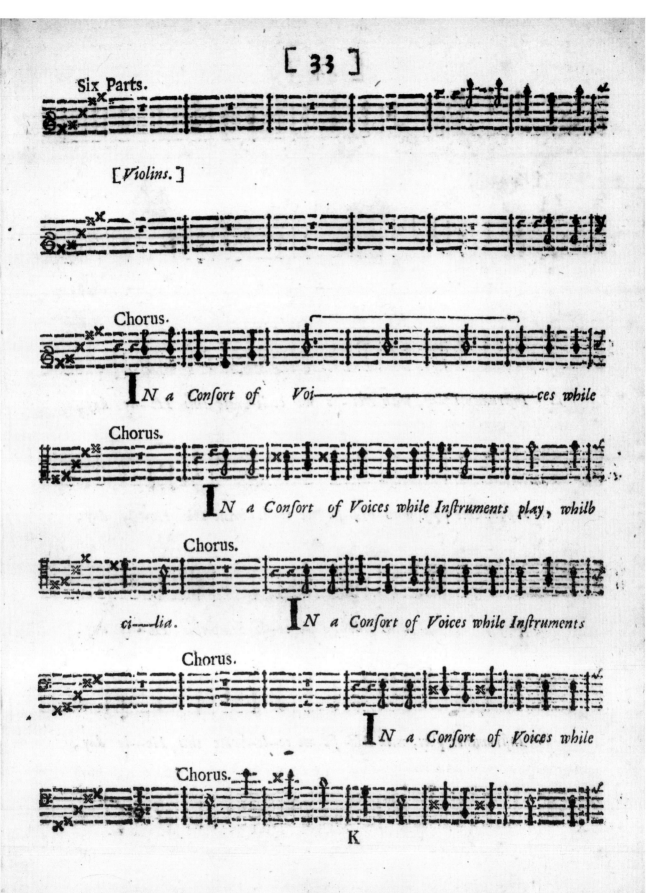

Six Parts.

[*Violins.*]

Chorus.

*I*N a Consort of Voi———————————ces while

Chorus.

*I*N a Consort of Voices while Instruments play, whilb

Chorus.

ci——lia. *I*N a Consort of Voices while Instruments

Chorus.

*I*N a Consort of Voices while

Chorus.

K

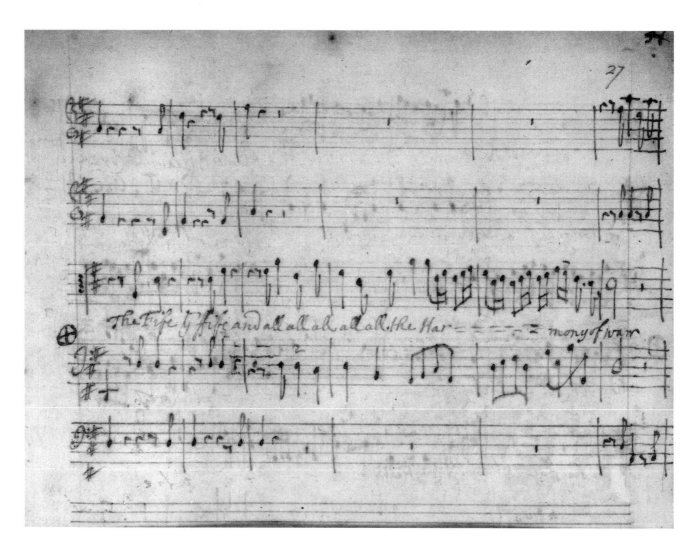

The Fife by Fife and all all all all all all the Har mony of war

46. A copy of Purcell's 'Hail, bright Cecilia' made by William Isaac of Windsor. (BL Add. MS.31453 f.27r)

harmony, from heavenly harmony' was set by Giovanni Battista Draghi, an Italian composer and keyboard virtuoso who had settled in London some twenty years previously. 'From harmony' uses five-part strings with solo passages, trumpets and recorders and is on an altogether grander scale: it seems to have caught Purcell's imagination, and many of his major works written after 1687 reflect its influence, beginning with 'Now does the glorious day appear', the first birthday ode for Queen Mary. Trumpets are introduced in 'Of old when heroes thought it base' of 1690, not a court ode but a 'Feast Song' composed for the annual London dinner of a society of Yorkshire gentlemen, who are said to have spent £100 on its performance. Purcell was again invited to compose the St Cecilia ode in 1692, and his 'Hail, bright Cecilia' is perhaps the most ambitious of all his non-theatrical works, with an orchestra including recorders (one of them a bass), oboes, trumpets and kettledrums: this work survives in a partial autograph and also in scores made for revivals, such as a copy made in January 1700 by William Isaac of Windsor (fig.46). The large crosses placed against the continuo bass line, which lies above the kettledrum part, may mean that the score was used by a keyboard player who found it difficult to break the habit of looking at the bottom stave.

The keyboard manuscript

In 1994 an oblong folio book of keyboard music containing, at one end, music by Purcell copied in his own hand and, at the other, autograph music by Giovanni Battista Draghi was sold at Sotheby's for £276,500. Generous donations enabled the British Library to match this sum and purchase the book, which the Library has catalogued as MS.Mus.1., in 1995. The manuscript is the only source of a number of works by both Purcell and Draghi, and of hitherto unknown arrangements of other pieces by Purcell, such as a keyboard version of the Hornpipe from *The Fairy Queen* (Plate VII). Two suites in A minor and C major later published in *A Choice Collection* are included in variant versions with movements that do not appear in the printed edition, and Purcell also copied Orlando Gibbons's G major prelude from *Parthenia* of 1612/13.

It is unlikely that the two composers collaborated in copying the music, and the book probably belonged to a pupil or pupils who took lessons from Purcell between 1693 and 1695 before later studying with Draghi: Purcell is known to have had a number of harpsichord pupils in the 1690s and Draghi was a well-known virtuoso who might well have been employed to teach an advanced student. The music copied by Purcell varies considerably in difficulty and is not laid out in a progressive order, so he perhaps used the book for teaching related pupils who were at different stages, possibly Annabella Howard, the youthful fourth wife of Sir Robert Howard, and Sir Robert's little granddaughter Diana. Annabella was certainly one of Purcell's pupils and payments to Purcell in the Howard family accounts for 'teaching Miss on the Harpsichord' could refer to Diana, who lived in Sir Robert's household.

Draghi was generally known as 'Mr Baptist' and on one of the end pages he set directions to his house to a melody: 'In Bedford street over against ye Cross Keys Tavern at ye Signe of ye Catt – Baptist'. Aristocratic pupils were probably taught in their own homes, but the directions may have been for a servant to deliver the book to Draghi so that a new piece of music could be written in it. The manuscript is an important source of Draghi's keyboard music and the only known example of his autograph.

Past Master

Purcell seems to have flourished in a kind of musical democracy, none of his achievements being due to exclusive patronage or a lack of opportunity given to others. Of the nine anthems performed at the 1685 coronation, for example, he composed only the first and the last; three were by John Blow, two by William Turner and one apiece by Henry Lawes and William Child. The majority of his works to appear in print in his lifetime did so in anthologies alongside the music of other composers. As far as we can tell his colleagues admired him as a musician and liked him as a man, and there is no reason to doubt the sincerity of the many elegies written after his death, though a more meaningful tribute might be the successive editions of *Orpheus Britannicus* (Plate VI). *Orpheus* amounts to a comprehensive survey of Purcell's art as a song composer

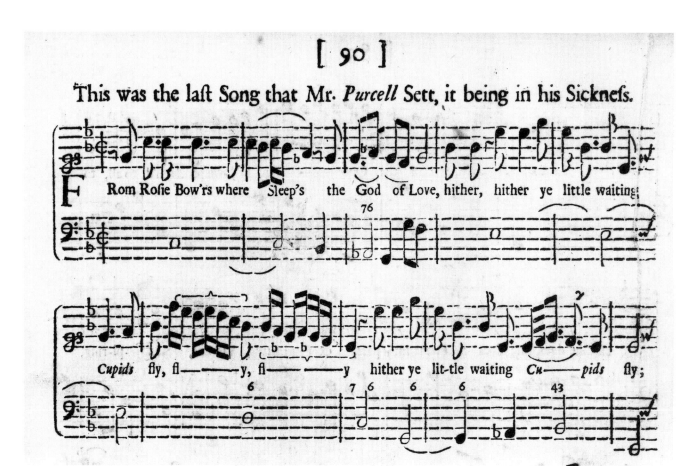

[90]

This was the laſt Song that Mr. *Purcell* Sett, it being in his Sickneſs.

Rom Roſie Bow'rs where Sleep's the God of Love, hither, hither ye little waiting

Cupids fly, fl————y, fl————y hither ye lit-tle waiting Cu————pids fly;

47. Purcell's last composition: 'From rosy bowers' as it was printed in *Orpheus Britannicus* I, 1698. (BL Music Library G.100. p.90)

from the 1680s to 'From rosy bowers' of 1695, 'the last Song that Mr Purcell Sett, it being in his Sickness' (fig.47).

There is abundant evidence that in his thirties Purcell became a genuinely popular composer, providing different kinds of music for amateur as well as professional musicians and exploiting his major works so that parts of them at least reached the widest possible audience. No longer able to look forward to a lifetime of court patronage, Purcell had to turn to a wider public, apparently relishing rather than resenting the new situation: his additions to the 1694 and subsequent editions of Playford's *Introduction to the Skill of Musick*, the principal popular instruction book of the time, are written with as much apparent enthusiasm as competence and in no way suggest that work of this kind is beneath the dignity of an organist of Their Majesties' Chapel Royal. A single opening of this book shows both Purcell's readiness to acknowledge achievement by others and his consciousness of tradition. Page 114 of the 1697 edition shows an example of invertible counterpoint from an Italian sonata ascribed to Lelio Colista; it is in fact by Lonati, but all English sources of the time contain the same misattribution (fig.48). Opposite, on page 115, Purcell refers his readers to Elway Bevin's *A Briefe and Short Introduction of the Art of Musicke* of 1631 for instruction about canon.

Purcell's sense of the value of earlier music makes it especially appropriate that the most old-fashioned of his late works, the simple note-against-note setting of 'Thou

Of this fort, there are fome Fuges ufed by fe-
veral Authors in *Sonata's*; a fhort One I fhall here
infert of the famous *Lelio Califta*, an *Italian*.

In

48. John Playford's *Introduction to the Skill of Musick* as revised by Purcell. This is the 13th edition of 1697. (BL 1423.b.2 p.114)

knowest Lord' he composed for Queen Mary's funeral, came to be his memorial amongst professional musicians. In his anthem collection *Musica Sacra* of 1724 William Croft published a setting of the seven funeral sentences including Purcell's 'Thou knowest Lord' rather than a new version of his own, 'The reason', he writes in his introduction, being 'obvious to every artist'. BL Add. MS. 5054, one of the manuscripts that preserve 'Thou knowest Lord' with the older series of funeral sentences by Thomas Morley, also incorporates a setting of the seventh sentence by William Croft different from that published in 1724, so the funeral sentences sung at Purcell's burial may have included an earlier tribute from the young Croft. More established musicians composed extended memorial odes such as Jeremiah Clarke's 'Come, come along for a dance and a song', in which celebration turns to grief at the news of the composer's death, and John Blow's 'Mark how the lark and linnet sing' (fig.49).

The sorrow of Purcell's contemporaries was natural, but it would be a sad irony if three hundred years on we associated him primarily with his funeral music or thought of his life in terms of unfulfilled potential rather than actual achievement. The evidence of his manuscripts and music reveals an energetic, determined and lively character, never quite satisfied with what he had written and always ready to try something different; a composer with the confidence that comes from an intimate knowledge of instruments and voices, close friendship with expert performers and a profound understanding of traditional as well as modern techniques; and a man of lively intelligence and warm humanity. Henry Hall's elegy, which seems to end on a note of triumph, is perhaps a more fitting memorial than its author realised (fig.50).

OPPOSITE
49. The title page of 'Mark how the Lark and Linnet sing', an elegy for Purcell by Dryden set to music by John Blow. (BL Music Library G.105)

50. Part of Henry Hall's elegaic poem printed in *Orpheus Britannicus* I. (BL Music Library G.100. p.vi)

Hail ! and for ever hail Harmonious Shade !
I lov'd thee Living, and admire thee Dead.
Apollo's Harp at once our Souls did ftrike,
We learnt together, but not learnt alike :
Though equal care our Mafter might beftow,
Yet only *Purcell* e're fhall equal *Blow :* (fign'd,
For Thou, by Heaven for wondrous things de-
Left'ft thy Companion lagging far behind.

Sometimes a HERO in an Age appears ;
But fcarce a PURCELL in a Thoufand Years.

By *H. Hall,* Organift of *Hereford.*

AN
ODE,
ON THE
DEATH
OF
Mr. Henry Purcell;

Late Servant to his Majesty, and
Organist of the Chapel Royal,
and of St. *Peter's Westminster*.

The Words by Mr. *Dryden*, and Sett to
Musick by Dr. *Blow*.

LONDON,
Printed by *J. Heptinstall*, for *Henry Playford*, at his Shop
in the *Temple Change Fleetstreet*, or at his House in
Arundelstreet over against the Blew Ball. 1696.

Bibliography

For many years Purcell scholarship has rested on the works of Sir Jack Westrup and Franklin B. Zimmerman, but the tercentenary celebration has led to the publication of so many significant books and articles that a comprehensive list cannot be given here. Up to date bibliographies can be found in many of the recent books listed below. Purcell's complete works have been published by the Purcell Society in 32 volumes, many of which are available in new or revised editions: the introductions and commentaries in the more recent volumes by scholars such as Alan Browning, Thurston Dart, Peter Dennison, Nigel Fortune, Peter Holman, Margaret Laurie, Anthony Lewis, Andrew Pinnock, Ian Spink, Michael Tilmouth and Bruce Wood are essential sources of information.

The bibliography has also been used to give full citations for important early works and to list some of the early sources that have been published in facsimile.

Books

Adams, M. *Henry Purcell: the Origins and Development of his Musical Style* (Cambridge, 1995)
Ashbee, A. *Records of English Court Music* I, II (Snodland, 1986, 1987); V (Aldershot, 1991); VIII (1995)
Burden, M. (ed.) *The Purcell Companion* (London, 1995)
— *Performing the Music of Henry Purcell* (Oxford, 1995)
Campbell, M. *Henry Purcell, Glory of his Age* (London, 1993)
Duffy, M. *Henry Purcell* (London, 1994)
Holman, P. *Henry Purcell* (London, 1994)
— *Four and Twenty Fiddlers: the Violin at the English Court 1540-1690* (Oxford, 1993)
King, R. *Henry Purcell: a greater musical genius England never had* (London, 1994)
Krummel, D. W. *English Music Printing 1553-1700* (London, 1975)
Price, C. A. *Henry Purcell and the London Stage* (Cambridge, 1984)
— (ed.) *Purcell Studies* (Cambridge, 1995)
Sandford, F. *The History of the Coronation of the Most High, Most Mighty, and Most Excellent Monarch, James II* (London, 1687)
— *The Order and Ceremonies Used for, and at the Solemn Interment of the most High, Mighty and most Noble Prince George Duke of Albemarle* (London, 1670)
Westrup, J. A. *Purcell* (London, 1937: new ed. revised C. A. Price, 1995)

Zimmerman, F. B. *Henry Purcell, 1659-1695: his Life and Times* (2nd ed. Philadelphia, 1983)
— *Henry Purcell, 1659-1695: an Analytical Catalogue of his Music* (London, 1963)

Periodical articles and chapters in anthologies listed above to which specific reference has been made

Holman, P. 'Henry Purcell and Daniel Roseingrave: A New Autograph', *Purcell Studies* 94-105
Langhans, E. A. 'The Theatrical Background', *The Purcell Companion* 299-312
Parrott, A. 'Performing Purcell', *The Purcell Companion* 385-444
Price, C. A. 'Newly Discovered Autograph Keyboard Music of Purcell and Draghi', *Journal of the Royal Musical Association* 120 (1975), 77-111
Savage, R. 'The Theatre Music' *The Purcell Companion* 313-384
Shay, R. 'Purcell as Collector of "Ancient" Music: Fitzwilliam MS 88', *Purcell Studies* 35-50
Thompson, R. 'Purcell's Great Autographs', *Purcell Studies* 6-34
— 'Manuscript Music in Purcell's London', *Early Music* 1995
Wood, B. 'The First Performance of Purcell's Funeral Music for Queen Mary', *Performing the Music of Henry Purcell*

Facsimiles

The Gostling Manuscript with foreword by F. B. Zimmerman (Austin, Texas, 1977)
— *Henry Purcell: The Gresham Autograph* with introduction by Margaret Laurie and Robert Thompson (London, 1995)
Ogilby, J. and Morgan, W. *A Large and Accurate Map of the City of London* (1677): facsimile with introduction by Ralph Hyde (London, 1976)
Playford, J. *An Introduction to the Skill of Musick* 12th edn. (1694): facsimile with introduction by F. B. Zimmerman (New York, 1972)

Several facsimiles of seventeenth-century printed editions of music have been published, notably in the series *Music for London Entertainment 1660-1800*.

Autograph manuscripts by Henry Purcell in The British Library

This list contains details of British Library holdings of works in Purcell's autograph, together with the complete contents for R.M.20.h.8., in which some music was copied by assistants, presumably under Purcell's supervision. The list has been divided into four broad categories: sacred vocal music, secular vocal music, keyboard music and instrumental music and includes the numbers assigned by Franklin B. Zimmerman in *Henry Purcell, 1659-1695: an Analytical Catalogue of his Music* (London, 1963), together with a reference identifying the manuscript, and the folio number of the first page of music.

Key to manuscript numbers

Music Library Manuscripts
A   R.M.20.h.8.
B   MS.Mus.1.

Manuscripts in the Department of Manuscripts
C   Add MS.30930
D   Add MS.30931
E   Add MS.30932
F   Add MS.30934
G   Egerton MS.2956

Title	z no.	MS	Folio
SACRED VOCAL WORKS			
Ah! few and full of sorrows [incomplete]	z130	C	15v
Awake, and with attention hear	z181	A	169
Awake, put on thy strength (largely not *autograph*, incomplete)	z1	A	13v
Beati omnes qui timent Dominum	z131	C	11
Begin the song and strike the living lyre (fragment)	z183	A	128
Behold, now praise the Lord	z3	E	121
Blessed are they that fear the Lord	z5	D	61
Domine non est exaltatum cor meum [incomplete]	z102	C	13
Early, O Lord, my fainting soul	z132	C	26
Gloria Patri et Filio	z103	C	7v
Hear me O Lord, and that soon [incomplete]	z13A	C	23v
Hear me, O Lord, the great support	z133	C	28
I was glad when they said unto me	z19	A	25v
I will give thanks unto Thee, O Lord [nearly complete]	z20	A	48
In the midst of life	z17A	D	81v
In thee, O Lord, do I put my trust	z16	A	17v
It is a good thing to give thanks	z18	A	4
Jehova, quam multi sunt hostes	z135	C	8v
Let the night perish (Job's curse)	z191	A	211
Lord, I can suffer Thy rebukes	z136	C	22
Lord, not to us [incomplete]	z137	C	14
My beloved spake	z28	E	87
My heart is fixed, O God	z29	A	28v
My heart is inditing	z30	A	53v
O Lord, our Governor	z141	C	18
O praise God in His holiness	z42	A	7v
O, all ye people, clap your hands	z138	C	4
O, I'm sick of life	z140	C	20v
O sing unto the Lord (not *autograph*)	z44	A	67
Out of the deep have I called	z45	D	67
Plung'd in the confines of despair	z142	C	3
Praise the Lord, O Jerusalem (not *autograph*)	z46	A	75
Praise the Lord, O my soul, and all that is within me	z47	A	32v
Praise the Lord O my soul (not *autograph*, incomplete)	z48	A	81
Rejoice in the Lord alway (incomplete)	z49	A	37v
Since God so tender a regard	z143	C	24v
The Lord is my light	z55	A	22v
They that go down to the sea [incomplete]	z57	A	52
Thou know'st, Lord, the secrets of our hearts (first setting, first version)	z58A	D	83
Unto Thee will I cry, O Lord	z63	A	43
When on my sick bed I languish	z144	C	6
Who hath believed our report?	z64	E	94
Why do the heathen	z65	A	39v
With sick and famish'd eyes	z200	A	198v
SECULAR VOCAL MUSIC			
Above the tumults of a busy state	z480	A	217
Amidst the shades and cool refreshing streams	z355	A	210
Arise, my muse (not *autograph*, incomplete)	z320	A	90
Cease, anxious world, your fruitless pain (mostly *autograph*)	z362	A	175
Celestial music did the gods inspire (largely not *autograph*)	z322	A	125v
Draw near, you lovers	z462	A	211v
Fly bold rebellion	z324	A	197v
From hardy climes	z325	A	207
From those serene and rapturous joys	z326	A	182v
Go tell Amynta, gentle swain	z489	A	183v
Hark, Damon, hark	z541	A	218
Hark, how the wild musicians sing	z542	A	222v
Haste, gentle Charon	z490	A	215
Here's to thee, Dick (not *autograph*)	z493	A	157
How pleasant is this flow'ry plain	z543	A	226
If ever I more riches did desire	z544	A	144v

If pray'rs and tears	z380	A	172
In a deep vision's intellectual scene	z545	A	201
In some kind dream	z497	A	169v
Laudate Ceciliam	z329	A	190
No, to what purpose should I speak	z468	A	212v
Now does the glorious day appear (not *autograph*)	z332	A	116v
O solitude, my sweetest choice (partly *autograph*)	z406	A	174
O! what a scene does entertain my sight	z506	A	188
Of old when heroes thought it base ('Yorkshire Feast Song')			
(*autograph*)	z333	G	1
(not *autograph*)	z333	A	105v
See where she sits	z508	A	209
Soft notes and gently rais'd accent	z510	A	185v
Sound the trumpet, beat the drum	z335	A	139
Swifter, Isis, swifter flow	z336	A	245v
Sylvia, thou brighter eye of night	z511	A	184v
The summer's absence unconcerned we bear	z337	A	232v
They say you're angry (not *autograph*)	z422	A	174v
This poet sings the Trojan wars	z423	A	140
Though my mistress be fair	z514	A	186v
Underneath this myrtle shade	z516	A	213v
We reap all the pleasures (incomplete)	z547	A	224
What shall be done in behalf of the man	z341	A	238
When Teucer from his father fled	z522	A	173
While you for me alone had charms	z524	A	216
Who can from joy refrain?	z342	F	80
Why, why are all the muses mute	z343	A	166
Ye tuneful muses, raise your heads (not *autograph*)	z344	A	155

KEYBOARD MUSIC

The Double Dealer		B	
Minuet	z592/7 var		2v
Air	z592/9 var		3v
The Old Bachelor – Hornpipe	z607/4 var	B	3
The Virtuous Wife		B	
Trumpet minuet	z611/8 var		6v
Air, 'La Furstenburg'	z611/9 var		7
Minuet	z611/7 var		
The Fairy Queen		B	
Hornpipe	z629/1b var		5v
Thus happy and free	z629/44a var		2v
Suite in A minor		B	
Prelude	z663/1 var		8
Almand	z663/2 var		8v
Corant	z663/3 var		9v
Jig	–		10
Suite in C		B	
Prelude	–		1v
Minuet	–		2
Air	–		2
Suite in C		B	
Prelude	–		10v
Almand	z666/2 var		11
Corant	z666/3 var		11v
Sarraband	z666/4 var		12

INSTRUMENTAL MUSIC

Chacony [à 4 in g]	z730	C	56
Fantazia, '3 parts upon a Ground' [fragment]	z731	E	121
Fantazias à 3		C	
in d	z732		71
in F	z733		70v
in g	z734		69v
Fantazias à 4		C	
in g	z735		67
in B flat	z736		66
in F	z737		65
in c	z738		64
in d	z739		63
in a	z740		62
in e	z741		61
in G	z742		60
in d	z743		59
in a [incomplete]	z744		58
Fantazia upon one note [à 5 in F]	z745	C	50
In nomine à 6 in g	z746	C	48
In nomine à 7 in g	z747	C	46
Pavan à 4 in g	z752	C	57
Sonata I [b]	z802	C	43v
Sonata II [E flat]	z803	C	41v
Sonata III [a]	z804	C	39v
Sonata IV [d] [fragments]	z805	C	32,37*
Sonata VII [C]	z808	C	35v
Sonata VIII [g]	z809	C	34
Sonata IX ('The Golden') [F]	z810	C	37v
Sonata X [D]	z811	C	31
Suite in G	z770	C	
[Jigg] [incomplete]	z770/4		52v
[Minuet] [incomplete]	z770/3		53
[Borry] [incomplete]	z770/2		53
[Air] [= z597/4]	z770/1c		53v
Overture	z770/1a&b		54

Works listed by Purcell in the index of R.M.20.h.8. for which no music appears in the manuscript

I will give thanks unto the Lord	z21
O Lord, grant the King a long life	z38
The title of 'The Thraldome out of Mr Cowley (I came, I saw, and was undone)' z375 appears on f.170v	

Music by other composers copied by Purcell

John Blow, 'O pray for the peace of Jerusalem'	A	16v
Maurizio Cazzati, 'Crucior in hac flamma'	A	127
John Eccles? [Hornpipe or Scotch Tune]	B	6
Orlando Gibbons, Prelude [no.21 from *Parthenia*]	B	4
Pelham Humphrey, 'By the waters of Babylon'	E	52

List of exhibits

Abbreviations: CC = Christ Church, Oxford; ML = British Library, Music Library; NPG = National Portrait Gallery, London; PD = British Museum, Department of Prints and Drawings; PRO = Public Record Office, London.

Introduction

A PORTRAIT OF PURCELL. Attributed to John Closterman. NPG 4994

LONDON IN THE LATE SEVENTEENTH CENTURY. Anon: *Prospect of London, Southwark, Westminster and the Thames, from the North bank*. PD

A VIEW OF WESTMINSTER. Hendrick Dankerts: *Whitehall and Westminster from St James's Park*. PD

A BIRD'S-EYE VIEW OF WHITEHALL. Leonard Knyff. PD

Apprenticeship and early mastery: Purcell's career to 1682

WARRANTS TO PROVIDE CLOTHING AND MONEY FOR PURCELL: 17 DECEMBER 1673. PRO LC5/140 p.384

PURCELL'S EARLIEST MUSIC COPYING? Pelham Humfrey: 'By the waters of Babylon'. Additional MS.30932 f.53v

AN EARLY MANUSCRIPT OF PURCELL'S FUNERAL SENTENCES. Henry Purcell: 'In the midst of life', *autograph*. Additional MS.30931 f.81v

A FIGURED BASS MANUAL BY JOHN BLOW. John Blow: 'Rules for playing of a Through Bass upon Organ & Harpsicon'. Additional MS.34072 ff.1v-2r

HENRY PURCELL: 'JEHOVA QUAM MULTI SUNT HOSTES' COPIED BY JOHN BLOW. CC MS Mus 628, pp.135-6

AN ORGAN PART ARRANGED BY PURCELL. John Blow: 'God is our hope and strength'. CC MS Mus 554 f.3r

AN ANTHEM FOR WESTMINSTER ABBEY. Henry Purcell: 'Let God arise', *autograph* corrections. Westminster Abbey Triforium Set 1, contratenor cantoris book f.58v

WESTMINSTER ABBEY: PAYMENTS FOR COPYING IN 1677. Westminster Abbey Muniments 33712 f.5v

AN ANTHEM FOR THE CHAPEL ROYAL. Henry Purcell: 'My beloved spake'. Additional MS.50860 f.7r

A FANTAZIA BY PURCELL. Henry Purcell: three-part fantazia no.2 in F, second treble; title page of the companion bass partbook. Additional MS.31435 ff.34v-35r.

LOCKE'S AUTOGRAPH SCOREBOOK. Matthew Locke: fantasia in D minor, from the 'Consort of Four Parts', *autograph*. Additional MS.17801 ff.50v-51r

PURCELL'S ELEGY FOR MATTHEW LOCKE. Henry Purcell: 'What hope for us remains now he is gone?' from John Playford, *Choice Ayres and Songs ... the Second Book*, 1679. ML K.7.i.19.(4) pp.66-67

THE BARNARD COLLECTION. William Byrd (1543-1623): Anthem 'O Lord make thy servant' from John Barnard, *The First Book of Select Church Musick*. ML K.7.e.2. medius decani book f.115v

PURCELL AS EDITOR. William Byrd: 'O Lord make thy servant'. Fitzwilliam Museum, Cambridge, MU MS.88 ff.125r-124v (inverted)

PURCELL'S OWN COPY OF 'JEHOVA QUAM MULTI SUNT HOSTES'. Additional MS.30930 ff.8v-9r, *autograph*

PURCELL'S ADMISSION AS A GENTLEMAN OF THE CHAPEL ROYAL. PRO LS13/197 f.91v

The Glory of the Temple: 1682-88

CHARLES II. Studio of John Riley. NPG 3798

JAMES II. Sir Peter Lely. NPG 5211

A WELCOME SONG FOR CHARLES II. Henry Purcell: 'Swifter Isis, swifter flow'. Additional MS.33287 ff.78v-79r

THREE VIEWS OF THE THAMES BY WENCESLAUS HOLLAR. PD

THE FIRST COPY OF A PURCELL ANTHEM. Henry Purcell: 'I was glad', *autograph*. Barber Institute, University of Birmingham MS 5001 ff.154v-155r

A FAVOUR FOR A COLLEAGUE? Daniel Roseingrave: 'O Lord thou art become gracious'. CC MS Mus 1215

A CORONATION ANTHEM. Henry Purcell: 'My heart is inditing', *autograph*. ML R.M.20.h.8. ff.55v-56r

AN ANTHEM FOR A NATIONAL THANKSGIVING. Henry Purcell: 'Blessed are they that fear the Lord', *autograph*. Additional MS.30931 f.63r

LIST OF JAMES II'S PRIVATE MUSIC: 31 AUGUST 1685. PRO LC3/30 p.101

INSTRUCTIONS TO PAY PURCELL AS INSTRUMENT KEEPER, 1688. PRO T27/11 p.314

After the Glorious Revolution: church, court and chamber music 1689-95

WILLIAM III AND MARY II. After William Wissing (?). NPG 580 and 606.

A VIOLIN PART FOR AN ANTHEM. Henry Purcell: 'My song shall be alway', second violin part, partly *autograph*. CC MS Mus 1188-9 f.45r

A SCORE COPIED IN OXFORD. Henry Purcell: 'My song shall be alway'. Additional MS.17840 ff.30v-31r

PURCELL'S LAST COURT ODE. Henry Purcell: 'A song compos'd for the Duke of Gloucester's Birth Day' *autograph*. Additional MS.30934 ff.82v-83r

PORTRAIT OF THE DUKE OF GLOUCESTER. Robert White. PD

A SONG FROM QUEEN MARY'S BIRTHDAY ODE, 1694. Henry Purcell: 'Strike the Viol' *autograph*. Guildhall Library, London: Gresham autograph, ff.56v-57r

THE GENTLEMAN'S JOURNAL. Henry Purcell: 'Strike the viol', from *The Gentleman's Journal* III, May 1694. P.P.5255 p.137

A FUNERAL SENTENCE FOR QUEEN MARY. Henry Purcell: 'Thou knowest Lord the secrets of our hearts'. Harleian MS 7340 ff.264v-265r

The Glory of the Stage: music for the theatre

A SCENE DESCRIPTION, 1674. *The Tempest or the Enchanted Iland: a Comedy as it is now Acted at Their Majesties Theatre in Dorset Garden.* 644.g.70. p.1

DRAMATIC MUSIC BY MATTHEW LOCKE. Matthew Locke: *The English Opera; or the Vocal Musick in Psyche, with the Instrumental Therein Intermix'd … To which is Adjoyned the Instrumental Musick in The Tempest.* ML K.2.a.10. pp.68-69

OPERA IN THE FRENCH STYLE. Louis Grabu, *Albion and Albanius.* ML K.10.b.21. pp.296-7

THE CHACONNE FROM *DIOCLESIAN*. Henry Purcell, *the Vocal and Instrumental Musick of the Prophetess, or the History of Dioclesian.* ML Hirsch.II.754. pp.60-61

KING ARTHUR: STAGE DIRECTIONS FOR THE BEGINNING OF THE FROST SCENE. John Dryden: *King Arthur.* 11774.d.5. p.31

MUSIC FOR THE FROST SCENE. Henry Purcell: *King Arthur*, Act III. Additional MS.31447 f.33r

THE INDIAN QUEEN: INVOCATION OF THE GOD OF DREAMS. Henry Purcell: *The Indian Queen*, Act III. Additional MS.31449 ff.35v-36r

AUTUMN'S SONG FROM *THE FAIRY QUEEN*. Henry Purcell: *The Fairy Queen*, Act IV. Royal Academy of Music MS.3 ff.76v-77r

A MASQUE FOR THE ENTERTAINMENT OF THE KING. John Blow: *Venus and Adonis.* Additional MS.22100 ff.128v-129r

THE TEXT OF *DIDO AND AENEAS*. 'Nat.' [ie Nahum] Tate: *An Opera Perform'd at Mr. Josias Priest's Boarding-School at Chelsey.* Royal College of Music I.A.20 pp.6-7

Purcell and publishing

PURCELL'S 1683 SONATAS: PORTRAIT AND TITLE PAGE. Henry Purcell: *Sonnata's of III Parts.* ML K.4.g.10, first violin part

CONTRASTS OF STYLE IN THE 1683 SONATAS. Henry Purcell: Sonata VI. ML K.4.g.10, second violin part

JOHN PLAYFORD'S MUSIC HAND. William Gregory: four movements of a suite or sonata copied by John Playford. Additional MS.31430 ff.19v-20r

AN EVENING HYMN. Henry Purcell: 'Now that the Sun hath veil'd his Light' from *Harmonia Sacra* I, 1688. ML G.84. p.1

AYRES FROM *KING ARTHUR*. *A Collection of Ayres, Compos'd for the Theatre, and upon other Occasions*, 1697. ML K.4.i.10. pp.4-5

TWO CATCHES. Henry Playford, *The Pleasant Musical Companion*, 1701. ML A.412.e. nos 48-9

KEYBOARD MUSIC FOR AMATEURS. Henry Purcell: 'A new Irish tune' and 'Riggadoon' from Henry Playford, *The Second Part of Musick's Hand-maid*, 1689. ML K.4.b.10.(2)

PURCELL'S WILL. PRO PROB 1/8

Music for St Cecilia's Day

A SERMON IN PRAISE OF MUSIC. Sampson Estwick: *The Usefulness of Church Music*, 1696. 3478.c.19. p.1.

THE 1683 ST CECILIA ODE. Henry Purcell, *A Musical Entertainment perform'd on November XXII. 1683*, 1684. ML K.4.c.18. pp.32-33

DRAGHI'S ODE OF 1687. Giovanni Battista Draghi: 'From harmony, from heav'nly harmony'. West Sussex County Record Office MS Cap.VI/1/1 ff.21v-22r [= pp.40-41]

THE YORKSHIRE FEAST SONG. Henry Purcell: 'Of old when heroes thought it base', *autograph*. Egerton MS.2956 ff.1v-2r

THE 1692 ST CECILIA ODE. Henry Purcell, 'Hail, bright Cecilia'. Additional MS.31453 ff.26v-27r

MUSIC FOR THE ST CECILIA'S DAY SERVICE, 1694. Henry Purcell, *Te Deum & Jubilate*, 1697. ML Hirsch. IV.896. pp.6-7

The keyboard manuscript

THEATRE MUSIC IN A KEYBOARD ARRANGEMENT. Henry Purcell: keyboard version of the hornpipe from *The Fairy Queen: autograph.* ML MS.Mus.1. f.5v

A CHOICE COLLECTION. Henry Purcell, *A Choice Collection of Lessons for the Harpsichord or Spinnet*, 1696. ML K.1.c.5. pp.26-27

THE KING'S VIRGINALS. Cobbe collection of historical keyboard instruments, Hatchlands

Past Master

PURCELL'S LAST SONG. Henry Purcell, 'From rosy bowers', from *Orpheus Britannicus* I. ML G.100. pp.90-91

ORPHEUS BRITANNICUS I: TITLE PAGE AND PORTRAIT. Henry Purcell, *Orpheus Britannicus* I, 1698. ML 15.c.11 (2)

PURCELL AS THEORIST. John Playford, *An Introduction to the Skill of Music*, 1697. 1423.b.2. pp.114-15

THE MUSIC OF PURCELL'S FUNERAL? Additional MS.5054 ff.131v-132r

EVELYN'S DIARY: 30 MAY 1698. (From the second and last volume of John Evelyn's diary, covering the years 1697-1706, now in the Evelyn Archive at The British Library.)

Index

Index of manuscripts

All Soul's College, Oxford: 11,81: fig.29

Barber Institute, University of Birmingham: MS 5001: 18

Bodleian Library, Oxford: MS Mus.Sch. C.61: fig.21

British Library, London:
Add.MS.5054: 56
Add.MS.17840: 23
Add.MS.17801: 14
Add.MS.30930: 16, fig.11
Add.MS.30931: 12
Add.MS.30932: 12, fig.2
Add.MS.30934: 25, fig.23
Add.MS.31435: fig.8
Add.MS.31447: fig.35
Add.MS.31449: 18, 41
Add.MS.31453: fig.46
Add.MS.33287: fig.13
Add.MS.34072: fig.4
Add.MS.50860: 12
Harl.MS.7340: fig.25
Lansdowne MS.1171: figs 30,31
Music Library MS.Mus.1: 53, plate VIII
Music Library MS. R.M.20.h.8: 18, 22, 23, plate III
Map Library c.7.b.4: fig.27
Map Library CRACE PORT.II.58: fig.28

Christ Church, Oxford:
MS Mus 554: fig.5
MS Mus 628: 10, 11, 12, 14, 16
MS Mus 1188-9: fig.22
MS Mus 1215: fig.15

Fitzwilliam Museum, Cambridge: MU MS 88: 14, 16, fig.10

Guildhall Library, London: Gresham autograph: 24, fig.24

Oriel College, Oxford: MS U.a.37: 25

Public Record Office, London:
LC5/120: fig.1
LC7/3: fig.33
LS13/197: fig.12
PROB 1/8: 48
PROB 11/375: 13
T27/11: 23

Royal Academy of Music, London: MS 3: 41

Westminster Abbey, London: Triforium Set 1: fig.6

Index of persons

Albemarle, Duke of 25, fig.26
Aldrich, Henry: 'Hark the bonny Christ Church bells' fig.41
Anne, Princess 18, 24, 25
Banister, John: *Circe* 38
Barnard, John: *The First Book of Selected Church Musick* 14
Betterton, Thomas 41
Bevin, Elway: *A Briefe and Short Introduction of the Art of Musicke* 54
Byrd, William: 'O Lord make thy servant' 14, fig.10
Blow, John 7, 8, 10, 11, 12, 14, 16, 18, 53, fig.3
—*Amphion Anglicus* fig.3
—'Begin the Song' 49
—'God is our hope and strength' 11, 14, fig.5
—'God spake sometimes in visions' 22
—'Mark how the lark and linnet sing' 56, fig.49
—'O Lord, I have sinned' 14
—'Rules for playing of a Through Bass upon Organ & Harpsicon' 10, fig.4
—*Venus and Adonis* 41, 45
Bowen, James ('Jemmy') 41
Cambert, Robert: *Ariane, ou le mariage de Bacchus* 20, 38
Cazzati, Maurizio 18
Charles II, King 8
Child, William 53
Clarke, Jeremiah: 'Come, come along for a dance and a song' 56
Colista, Lelio 54
Cooke, Henry 8
Croft, William 56
— *Musica Sacra* 56
Cross, Letitia 41
Cross, Thomas 46
D'Urfey, Thomas: *New Poems* 45
Davenant, Sir William 31
—*Salmacida Spolia* 33, figs 30,31
—*The Siege of Rhodes* 31
Draghi, Giovanni Battista ('Mr Baptist') 52, 53
—autograph keyboard music 53
—'From harmony, from heavenly harmony' 49, 52
—music for *Psyche* 38
Dryden, John 38, 49, plate VII
—*King Arthur* fig.34
Evelyn, John 20
George, Prince of Denmark 18, 24
Gibbons, Christopher 14
Gibbons, Orlando 14
—*Parthenia* 53
Grabu, Louis 38
—*Albion and Albanius* 38

Hall, Henry 7, 8, 56
Heptinstall, John 46
Hingeston, John 8, 12-13, fig.7
Howard, Annabella 53
Howard, Diana 53
Howard, Robert 53
—*The Loves of Dido and Aeneas* 45
Humfrey, Pelham 8, 11, 12
—'By the waters of Babylon' 8, fig.2
Isaac, William 52
James II, King 18, 20, 23
James, Prince 20
Jones, Inigo 33, figs 30-31
Killigrew, Thomas 31
Lawes, Henry 53
Lee, Nathaniel: *Theodosius* 38
Locke, Matthew 14, 46, fig.9
—music for *The Tempest* and *Psyche* 38
Lonati, Carlo Ambrogio 54
Lowe, Edward 17
Lully, Jean-Baptiste 38
—*Cadmus et Hermione* 38
Mary II, Queen 23, 24, 52, 56, plate v
Mary of Modena, queen of James II 20, plate IV
Morgan, William 31
Morley, Thomas: funeral sentences 24-5, 56
North, Roger 31
Ogilby, John 31
de Passé, Crispin: *Compendium Operum Virgilianorum* fig.38
Pearson, William 46
Philips, Edward: *A New World of Words* 22
Player, John 13
Playford, John 46, fig.39
—*Choice Ayres and Songs … the Second Book* 46
—*Introduction to the Skill of Musick* 54, fig.48
Playford, Henry 46, 48
—*Harmonia Sacra* 48
—*The Second Book of the Pleasant Musical Companion* fig.41
—*The Second Part of Musick's Hand-maid* fig.42
Priest, Josias 45
—boarding school at Chelsea 45, fig.36
Purcell, Daniel 25, 41
—*The Judgement of Paris* 41
Purcell, Elizabeth 7, 13
Purcell, Frances 17, 48
Purcell, Henry
—autograph keyboard music 24, 53, plate VIII
—'Blessed are they that fear the Lord' 20
—*Bonduca* 41
—*A Choice Collection of Lessons for the Harpsichord* 48, 53
—*Circe* 41
—*A Collection of Ayres, Compos'd for the Theatre* 48
—*Don Quixote* 41
—*Dido and Aeneas* 38, 41, 45, fig.37
—*Dioclesian* 38, 41, 46

—*The Fairy Queen* 41, 53
—'From rosy bowers' 54, fig.47
—Funeral march and canzona 25
—'Gentle shepherds, you that know' 46
—'Hail, bright Cecilia' 52, fig.46
—*The Indian Queen* 18, 41
—'I was glad' 18
—'Jehova quam multi sunt hostes' 16, fig.11
—*King Arthur* 41, figs.34, 35
—'Let God arise' 12, fig.6
—*The Libertine* 41
—'Music for a while' 41
—'My beloved spake' 12
—'My heart is inditing' 18, 20-23, plate III
—'My song shall be alway' 23, figs 21, 22
—'Now does the glorious day appear' 52
—*Oedipus* 41
—'Of old when heroes thought it base' (The Yorkshire Feast Song) 52
—*Orpheus Britannicus* 48, 53-4, plate VI
—*Sonnata's of III Parts* (1683) 46, fig.40
—'Strike the viol' fig.24
—'Swifter Isis' 18, fig.13
—Te Deum and Jubilate in D 48, 49
—*Ten Sonata's in Four Parts* (1697) 48
—*Theodosius* 38
—'Thou knowest Lord', final setting 24, 25, 54, 56, fig.25
—*Timon of Athens* 41
—'Welcome to all the pleasures' 49, figs 44, 45
—'What hope for us remains now he is gone?', elegy for Matthew Locke, 14, 46
—'Who can from joy refrain' 23-4, fig.23
Purcell, Henry, the elder 7, 31
Purcell, Thomas 7
Roseingrave, Daniel 18
—'Lord thou art become gracious' 18, fig.15
Sandford, Francis 22
—*The History of the Coronation of … James II* fig.17
—*The Order of Ceremonies Used for, and at the Solemn Interment … of George Duke of Albemarle* fig.26
Settle, Elkanah: *The Empress of Morocco* 31, 38, fig.32
Shadwell, Thomas:
—*The Tempest* 31, 38
—*Psyche* 31, 38
Staggins, Nicholas: *Calisto* 38
Shirley, James: *Cupid and Death* 31
Tate, Nahum 45
Tucker, William 12, fig.6
Tudway, Thomas 25, fig.25
Turner, William 53
Walsh, John 41
William III, King 23
William, Duke of Gloucester 23, fig.18
Withey, Francis 23
Wren, Christopher 31